*To Walk and to Please God*

T0243659

**New Testament Theology**

Edited by Thomas R. Schreiner and Brian S. Rosner

*The Beginning of the Gospel: A Theology of Mark*, Peter Orr

*From the Manger to the Throne: A Theology of Luke*, Benjamin L. Gladd

*The Mission of the Triune God: A Theology of Acts*, Patrick Schreiner

*Ministry in the New Realm: A Theology of 2 Corinthians*, Dane C. Ortlund

*United to Christ, Walking in the Spirit: A Theology of Ephesians*, Benjamin L. Merkle

*Hidden with Christ in God: A Theology of Colossians and Philemon*, Kevin W. McFadden

*To Walk and to Please God: A Theology of 1 and 2 Thessalonians*, Andrew S. Malone

*The God Who Judges and Saves: A Theology of 2 Peter and Jude*, Matthew S. Harmon

*The Joy of Hearing: A Theology of the Book of Revelation*, Thomas R. Schreiner

# To Walk and to Please God

*A Theology of 1 and 2 Thessalonians*

Andrew S. Malone

WHEATON, ILLINOIS

*To Walk and to Please God: A Theology of 1 and 2 Thessalonians*

© 2024 by Andrew S. Malone

Published by Crossway
        1300 Crescent Street
        Wheaton, Illinois 60187

Cover design: Kevin Lipp

First printing 2024

Printed in the United States of America

Trade paperback ISBN: 978-1-4335-7831-1
ePub ISBN: 978-1-4335-7834-2
PDF ISBN: 978-1-4335-7832-8

---

**Library of Congress Cataloging-in-Publication Data**

Names: Malone, Andrew S., author.
Title: To walk and to please God : a theology of 1 and 2 Thessalonians / Andrew S. Malone.
Description: Wheaton, Illinois : Crossway, 2024. | Series: New Testament theology | Includes bibliographical references and index.
Identifiers: LCCN 2023022740 (print) | LCCN 2023022741 (ebook) | ISBN 9781433578311 (trade paperback) | ISBN 9781433578328 (pdf) | ISBN 9781433578342 (epub)
Subjects: LCSH: Bible. Thessalonians—Criticism, interpretation, etc. | Patience—Religious aspects—Christianity.
Classification: LCC BS2725.52 .M335 2024 (print) | LCC BS2725.52 (ebook) | DDC 227/.8106—dc23/eng/20240102
LC record available at https://lccn.loc.gov/2023022740
LC ebook record available at https://lccn.loc.gov/2023022741

---

| VP | | | 33 | 32 | 31 | 30 | 29 | 28 | 27 | 26 | 25 | 24 |
|----|----|----|----|----|----|----|----|----|----|----|----|----|
| 15 | 14 | 13 | 12 | 11 | 10 | 9 | 8 | 7 | 6 | 5 | 4 | 3 | 2 | 1 |

To Erin and Zoe

*Now may our God and Father himself,*
*and our Lord Jesus,*
*direct our way to you,*
*and may the Lord make you increase*
*and abound in love for one another and for all,*
*as we do for you,*
*so that he may establish your hearts*
*blameless in holiness before our God and Father,*
*at the coming of our Lord Jesus with all his saints.*

1 THESSALONIANS 3:11–13

# Contents

# Illustrations

**Figures**

# Series Preface

THERE ARE REMARKABLY FEW treatments of the big ideas of single books of the New Testament. Readers can find brief coverage in Bible dictionaries, in some commentaries, and in New Testament theologies, but such books are filled with other information and are not devoted to unpacking the theology of each New Testament book in its own right. Technical works concentrating on various themes of New Testament theology often have a narrow focus, treating some aspect of the teaching of, say, Matthew or Hebrews in isolation from the rest of the book's theology.

The New Testament Theology series seeks to fill this gap by providing students of Scripture with readable book-length treatments of the distinctive teaching of each New Testament book or collection of books. The volumes approach the text from the perspective of biblical theology. They pay due attention to the historical and literary dimensions of the text, but their main focus is on presenting the teaching of particular New Testament books about God and his relations to the world on their own terms, maintaining sight of the Bible's overarching narrative and Christocentric focus. Such biblical theology is of fundamental importance to biblical and expository preaching and informs exegesis, systematic theology, and Christian ethics.

The twenty volumes in the series supply comprehensive, scholarly, and accessible treatments of theological themes from an evangelical perspective. We envision them being of value to students, preachers, and interested laypeople. When preparing an expository sermon series, for example, pastors can find a healthy supply of informative commentaries, but there are few options for coming to terms with the overall teaching of each book of the New Testament. As well as being useful in sermon and Bible study preparation, the volumes will also be of value as textbooks in college and seminary exegesis classes. Our prayer is that they contribute to a deeper understanding of and commitment to the kingdom and glory of God in Christ.

Tucked away at the tail end of Paul's congregation-focused correspondence, 1 and 2 Thessalonians might easily be regarded as truncated versions of the more famous and longer epistles. Dispelling this misunderstanding, Andrew Malone's engaging volume on Paul's Thessalonian letters reveals their immense value for understanding our lives as Christians and worshiping the true and living God. Here we find a remarkably comprehensive treatment of the Christian journey, from Paul and his coworkers' first steps of planting and nurturing a church through what it means to come to faith to living in consistency with our new identity in Christ and persevering to the end. All this is set within Paul's most overt and compelling teaching about the completion of our salvation at the return of Christ. Malone shows how the two letters offer every Christian great assistance in learning how "to walk and to please God."

Thomas R. Schreiner and Brian S. Rosner

# Acknowledgments

PRAISE BE TO GOD for the first church in Thessalonica. How encouraging it is to watch his effective work among these young believers, maturing them from his first calling and strengthening them to endure with a view to the return of Jesus. It is a privilege for us to study and learn from his labors and theirs.

I am grateful to many scholars who have already delved into these letters in far more depth than this modest volume permits. I have chosen to interact more regularly with commentators, Pauline specialists, and systematic theologians of the last two decades, who, in turn, have clearly benefited from those who preceded them. (Zondervan Academic kindly provided a preview of Seyoon Kim's Word Biblical Commentary volume, even though I was unable to engage it extensively.) I hope to have faithfully showcased something of their industry. Like a judicious sample container of chocolates or other confectionaries, I trust I have given readers an adequate taste of the many options available, raised awareness, and enticed further investment. I am especially satisfied if this exploration of Thessalonian themes results in greater interest in and use of these two letters themselves.

Sections of this book have been improved by input from Mike Bird, Mark Burbidge, Matthew Halsted, Scott Harrower, Matthew Jensen, and Andy Judd. (Several of these could be addressed as professor. At least one wants to be known as supreme leader.) I have received additional encouragement and input from my coworkers in ministry at Ridley College. And I am indebted to the leadership and board of the college for their generous sabbatical program, which facilitated much of my research and writing. Finally, the series editors and the publishing staff at Crossway have professionally shepherded the finished product.

Andrew Malone

# Abbreviations

| | |
|---|---|
| AB | Anchor Bible |
| *ANF* | *Ante-Nicene Fathers* |
| *BBR* | *Bulletin for Biblical Research* |
| BECNT | Baker Exegetical Commentary on the New Testament |
| BETL | Bibliotheca Ephemeridum Theologicarum Lovaniensium |
| BNTC | Black's New Testament Commentaries |
| BST | Bible Speaks Today |
| BTFL | Biblical Theology for Life |
| BTNT | Biblical Theology of the New Testament |
| *CTJ* | *Calvin Theological Journal* |
| *DPL*[1] | *Dictionary of Paul and His Letters.* Edited by Gerald F. Hawthorne and Ralph P. Martin. 1st ed. Downers Grove, IL: InterVarsity Press; Leicester, UK: Inter-Varsity Press, 1993. |
| *DPL*[2] | *Dictionary of Paul and His Letters.* Edited by Scot McKnight, Lynn H. Cohick, and Nijay K. Gupta. 2nd ed. Downers Grove, IL: IVP Academic, 2023. |
| FET | Foundations of Evangelical Theology |
| IVPNTC | InterVarsity Press New Testament Commentary |
| *JETS* | *Journal of the Evangelical Theological Society* |
| JSNTSup | Journal for the Study of the New Testament Supplement Series |

| | |
|---|---|
| NCB | New Century Bible |
| NCCS | New Covenant Commentary Series |
| *NDBT* | *New Dictionary of Biblical Theology.* Edited by T. Desmond Alexander and Brian S. Rosner. Leicester, UK: Inter-Varsity Press; Downers Grove, IL: InterVarsity Press, 2000. |
| NIBCNT | New International Biblical Commentary on the New Testament |
| NICNT | New International Commentary on the New Testament |
| *NIDOTTE* | *New International Dictionary of Old Testament Theology and Exegesis.* Edited by Willem A. VanGemeren. 5 vols. Grand Rapids, MI: Zondervan, 1997. |
| NIGTC | New International Greek Testament Commentary |
| NIVAC | New International Version Application Commentary |
| NSBT | New Studies in Biblical Theology |
| NTT | New Testament Theology (Crossway) |
| NTTh | New Testament Theology (Cambridge University Press) |
| PNTC | Pillar New Testament Commentary |
| SGBC | Story of God Bible Commentary |
| SP | Sacra Pagina |
| THNTC | Two Horizons New Testament Commentary |
| WBC | Word Biblical Commentary |
| WBT | Word Biblical Themes |
| WUNT | Wissenschaftliche Untersuchungen zum Neuen Testament |
| ZCINT | Zondervan Critical Introductions to the New Testament |
| ZECNT | Zondervan Exegetical Commentary on the New Testament |
| *ZNW* | *Zeitschrift für die neutestamentliche Wissenschaft und die Kunde der älteren Kirche* |

Introduction

# A Church in Good Standing

SO MUCH OF BIBLICAL STUDIES involves comparing and contrasting. As we witness the transition from the old covenant to the new covenant, which of God's interactions with humanity remain the same, and which aspects of his game plan are expressed differently? The same applies to the way we learn, not least to the way we learn about the Bible. We venture into new topics by comparing and contrasting them with what's already familiar to us. As Paul Ellingworth puts it, "We understand something new only in relation to other things that we know already."[1]

## An Underknown Church

Thinking about the paired tools of comparing and contrasting is a useful way to approach 1 and 2 Thessalonians. Of course, some Christians know these letters well. But I suspect that for many of us, venturing into these letters is like visiting a nearby country that speaks the same language. Whether it's Americans visiting Canada, Australians visiting New Zealand, or neighboring nations visiting Switzerland or Kenya or China, there is plenty that's almost like home—but there are enough sights and sounds that are sufficiently foreign to remind us that we are somewhere else. In tourism and in

---

1  Paul Ellingworth, "Hebrews and the Anticipation of Completion," *Themelios* 14, no. 1 (1988): 6.

biblical studies, it can be the minor differences amid major similarities that cause culture shock. We make mistakes when we fail to expect and respond to these differences.

By accident of length, the Thessalonian correspondence falls at the end of Paul's congregation-focused letters. When we approach Paul in canonical order, we have already been exposed to Romans, two letters to the Corinthians, Galatians, Ephesians, Philippians, and Colossians: more than five dozen chapters.

By accident of historical focus, many of those longer letters are on higher rotation in evangelical churches and seminaries. Romans and Galatians are prize exhibits from the Protestant Reformation and remain at the heart of much teaching about salvation. The Corinthian letters are popular in churches wanting to correct believers' behavior (though I'm sure 1 Corinthians is used more than 2 Corinthians). Ephesians invites us to glory in God's magnificent work in salvation, Colossians lets us thump the pulpit again as we warn against syncretistic heresies, and Philippians returns to practical advice for Christian behavior. When seeking guidance on church leadership, we leap ahead to the instructions addressed to Timothy and Titus.

The Thessalonian letters thus languish in an unfortunate position. They are like the eighth and ninth shops offering similar products after we've browsed the preceding seven or yet two more tourist stops after we've exhausted ourselves exploring the prior attractions along the route.

The language of tourist routes may also describe our reading of Acts. The founding of the church in Thessalonica in Acts 17:1–9 is often not a highlighted destination in a preacher's itinerary. It lacks the detail and drama of Philippi in the preceding chapter (Acts 16:11–40). The rest of Acts 17 gives glimpses of the faithful, Bible-studying Bereans (Acts 17:10–12) and of the evangelistic contextualizing of the gospel message for pagan intellectuals in Athens (Acts 17:16–34). Apart from a single verse promoting some success, the Thessalonian encounter can feel like (1) an odd regression into Old Testament territory when the gospel is supposed to be bursting into Gentile Europe or (2) rather ambivalent in terms of the gospel's progress, if not (3) an outright failure of the gospel to gain newsworthy traction, especially when compared with more stimulating "power encounters" and "triumphs" in Philippi and Corinth and Ephesus in surrounding chapters. (Even if some of those locations present mixed success, I wonder if we warm to them more because of our familiarity with subsequent letters to their churches.) We could well misunderstand Luke's purposes for each narrative. Unless we are disciplined or exhaustive in our reading and preaching programs, the events in Thessalonica are unlikely to make our highlight reel.[2]

### An Underappreciated Church?

In addition to these external factors, I wonder if the content of the Thessalonian letters also contributes to their neglect. Perhaps they are too autobiographical: modern congregants and their preachers want to hear more about *believers'* conduct than about the past practices of church planters. Perhaps they are too repetitive or too short: when we *do* care about church-planting practices, we have already scrutinized the longer details in the Corinthian correspondence. Perhaps the sense is that this congregation is too passive: they may appear as the set dressing against which the authors speak of their own past labors. Perhaps the tone is too sedentary: as with the bland Thessalonian narrative in Acts, we may prefer vibrant contention about spiritual gifts or robust doctrinal dispute or scandalous ethical misconduct. Perhaps the Thessalonian church is simply too uncontroversial: some modern churches, and especially some preachers, want something fiery like 1 Corinthians or Galatians to jolt miscreants from their complacency.

Both the external and internal factors are reminiscent of an urban legend about the demise of the great library at Alexandria. The

---

2   To be fair, Thessalonica barely makes Luke's highlight reel. He commonly starts a new missionary venture with a detailed description (such as Philippi's) that serves as a paradigm for any subsequent destinations (such as Thessalonica). For an example of Luke's paradigmatic approach, see Patrick Schreiner, *The Mission of the Triune God: A Theology of Acts*, NTT (Wheaton, IL: Crossway, 2022), 119–24.

attacking general allegedly decreed that if the library's books challenged the invaders' established worldview, then they were dangerous and should be destroyed, and if the books merely reiterated that worldview, then they were superfluous anyway. I wonder if this is how many of us approach 1 and 2 Thessalonians. Assuming these letters are truncated versions of what we've already mastered in Paul's more established epistles, why would we revisit another, shorter remix? (Once we've viewed a director's extended cut of a movie, how often are we attracted to an "incomplete" draft?) While few believers would suggest that anything in Thessalonians conflicts with other Pauline writings, I am confident that any alleged discrepancies would be resolved in favor of the more ingrained letters.[3]

### Compare and Contrast

I hope I have overstated my fear of Thessalonian neglect. But I've done so in order to alert us to any conscious or unconscious resistance we might face in reading the letters for ourselves or in sharing them with others.

### *This Book's Approach*

A consideration of how we compare and contrast letters also introduces the approach of this book. An author like me must walk a tightrope. How much should I encourage the study of Thessalonians because the two letters clearly *affirm* much of what we read elsewhere in Paul and the rest of the Bible? How much should I highlight the distinctive *differences* the Thessalonian epistles contribute? There is even a third, intermediate option: How much should I emphasize those elements that do both, that reinforce and *elaborate* on concepts found elsewhere? With an eye to Ellingworth's quote in the opening paragraph above, I am attempting all of these! I want to assure us that

---

3   John Byron opens his commentary lamenting that "in some ways, Thessalonians is the *stepchild* of the Pauline corpus." He partly blames this on "the absence of any of the theological themes that helped spur the Reformation." *1 and 2 Thessalonians*, SGBC 13 (Grand Rapids, MI: Zondervan, 2014), 1 (emphasis added).

the Thessalonian correspondence deserves a hearing because of its consistency with the rest of the canon. I want to promote those elements that extend our understanding of particular concepts. And of course, we must pay special attention to those unique contributions that God gifts to us only in these two books of the Bible. Comparing and contrasting is core to biblical theology—the method emphasized in this series—and it excels at allowing each canonical book its own voice.[4]

This kind of balance also plays out in the ranges chosen for such comparison and contrast. Obviously, I wish to show how Thessalonians accords with and contributes to the Pauline corpus (in which I include all thirteen letters traditionally associated with the apostle). In turn, I want to draw connections with the other letters beyond Paul's—which themselves can suffer from being placed and promoted behind the apostle's. The rest of the New Testament's teaching about the triune God and his plans warrants occasional mentions of the remaining books. Such a balance must necessarily dwindle for each successive range, as reflected in my Scripture index. That index also witnesses scant interaction with the Old Testament, a disappointing necessity. Chapter 4 shows that the writers and readers of the Thessalonian letters were not unfamiliar with what was, for them, the *entirety* of God's written revelation. But in contrast with other letters such as Romans and Hebrews, Old Testament doctrines and images are not a substantial tool in the epistolary nurture of the Thessalonian church.

I must also mention my openness to treating the two Thessalonian letters together, as do a good many studies. When it comes to synthesizing two letters with the same senders and recipients that were written bare months apart, we ought not to be surprised to find significant overlap in their themes and emphases.

4  Predetermined systematic theological categories can "flatten the unique shape of the individual canonical books and obscure their dynamic theology." Richard Schultz, "Integrating Old Testament Theology and Exegesis," in *NIDOTTE* 1:186.

Because we are rarely working systematically through either letter, it will aid readers to regularly read through the biblical text. It's the Bible's own words that this volume aims to illuminate and serve and that retain authority over scholarly insights and syntheses. Likewise, in only some places do I have the luxury of unpacking passages in as much detail as commentaries can.

*Coming Attractions*

By previewing our pending discoveries here, I can highlight major contributions of 1 and 2 Thessalonians. I have necessarily organized these into categories for readability, but I trust their selection is governed by the letters' own emphases.

The letters foreground the extended nature of the Christian journey. The Thessalonian epistles devote significant space to talking about how believers come to initial saving faith and to considering the conduct expected of them as they persevere through earthly life. Thessalonians also presents some of Paul's most overt teaching about how the triune God will once again intervene directly in his world to wrap up its present existence. These stages include some insightful theological elements, but these are not raised to stroke intellectual curiosity or to ignite doctrinal controversies or to fuel end-times speculation but to *pastor* Christians at every step. Believers at all stages of their Christian journey are invited to map their own progress and to encourage others in persevering.

As much as any of the other letters associated with Paul, Thessalonians gives us a number of detailed insights into the practices and emphases of Paul's team and their initial steps of planting and nurturing a church. Those workers involved today in related ministries are encouraged to explore which ingredients remain relevant, including the place of every-member ministry.

Everyday believers, church leaders, and scholars alike are concerned to understand Paul's comprehension of the triune God, on whose behalf they minister. Thessalonians contributes both consistent and surprising features, especially to the full divinity of the Lord Jesus Christ through prayers directed to him.

And unsurprisingly and reassuringly, we observe how all these contributions align with, extend, or make more accessible some of the contents of the other Pauline letters. Some topics, such as the life cycle or journey of a Christian believer, benefit from being compressed in these shorter letters. We can especially relate to ministry topics because the church at Thessalonica was largely composed of Gentile members, who are then nurtured through "Gentile" arguments. For those who trace any development in the doctrines and practices of Paul and of the early church, it is significant that the two Thessalonian letters are among the first extant writings of the New Testament. Galatians may have been composed earlier, but even if so, we have before us the next earliest records of God's new covenant church written only a year or two later.[5] At the same time, we dare not misjudge Paul and his team as novice theologians or even novice authors. These are merely among the first of their preserved letters, written in light of substantial experience. As Douglas Moo observes, "A decade and a half of study, preaching, and interaction with other believers was behind Paul before he first put quill to parchment."[6]

## Assumptions about Authorship and Structure

Evangelical commentators generally agree that both Thessalonian letters were written shortly after the church was founded, placing them around AD 51. Some skeptical scholars wonder if the second letter was a forgery written years later, but I fail to be persuaded by one of the core arguments, that the letters are *so* alike that one must have been plagiarized.

5   Conservative commentaries of the last few decades favor Galatians being written before the events of Acts 15 and thus before Paul's subsequent missionary journey with the founding of the Thessalonian church and the penning of its correspondence. Commentators continue to commend the detailed analysis of Richard N. Longenecker, *Galatians*, WBC 41 (Dallas: Word, 1990), lxxii–lxxxviii.

6   Douglas J. Moo, *A Theology of Paul and His Letters: The Gift of the New Realm in Christ*, BTNT (Grand Rapids, MI: Zondervan Academic, 2021), 9–10.

I am sympathetic, though, to interpreters who take seriously that there are three named collaborators. (Multiple authors appear in most of Paul's other congregation-focused letters; the most frequent coauthor is Timothy, as also here in Thessalonians.) Most commentators view these figures simply as associates in Paul's church-planting ministry who made little significant contribution to the writing of the letters. But Randolph Richards argues attractively and persuasively that letters could be composed corporately. While we may sometimes envision Paul as a solo apostle scribbling away with his feather quill or dictating to a scribe, it is entirely plausible to contemplate these letters as "the product of a committee."[7] The two Thessalonian letters speak almost exclusively in the plural— at least 148 terms concerning "we" and "us"—with Paul only five times interjecting in the singular as the authoritative team leader (1 Thess. 2:18; 3:5; 5:27; 2 Thess. 2:5; 3:17).[8] Several commentators lean in the "committee" direction, even if convenience or tradition often sees them revert to "Paul" as a shorthand.[9] Taking the letters' language as intentionally inclusive, I resist this convenience and strive to speak of all three contributors. This still permits Paul to

7  E. Randolph Richards, *Paul and First-Century Letter Writing: Secretaries, Composition, and Collection* (Downers Grove, IL: InterVarsity Press, 2004), 32–36; cf. 45–46, 103–8, 118–21, and elsewhere. "Committee" language is from Ben Witherington III, who dislikes this scenario but still allows the possibility of group input. *1 and 2 Thessalonians: A Socio-Rhetorical Commentary* (Grand Rapids, MI: Eerdmans, 2006), 47.

8  Abraham J. Malherbe notes these frequencies, though he seeks a different explanation of the myriad plurals. *The Letters to the Thessalonians: A New Translation with Introduction and Commentary*, AB 32B (New York: Doubleday, 2000), 86.

9  Stronger supporters include Gene L. Green, *The Letters to the Thessalonians*, PNTC (Grand Rapids, MI: Eerdmans, 2002), 56–59; Gordon D. Fee, *The First and Second Letters to the Thessalonians*, NICNT (Grand Rapids, MI: Eerdmans, 2009), 4, 13–14. Supporters with less detail include F. F. Bruce, *1 & 2 Thessalonians*, WBC 45 (Waco, TX: Word, 1982), 6, 11; Gary S. Shogren, *1 & 2 Thessalonians*, ZECNT 13 (Grand Rapids, MI: Zondervan, 2012), 55, 243. Others who see Silvanus and Timothy more as "cosenders" than "coauthors" often still allow some degree of contribution. The view of plural contributors can be found in prior generations, e.g., Origen, *Commentary on Matthew* 14.1 (ca. AD 250), in *ANF* 9:495; John Calvin, *1 & 2 Thessalonians* (ca. AD 1550), Crossway Classic Commentaries (Wheaton, IL: Crossway, 1999), 17 (on 1:1); E. H. Harrison, "'I' and 'We' in the Thessalonian Epistles," *The Expositor*, 8th ser., vol. 1, no. 2 (1911): 149–59.

lead the team and to authorize key points if not also the final form of the letters. Similarly, just as the letters are comfortable to describe Silvanus and Timothy as "apostles," I use this broader title for them (see 1 Thess. 2:6/7).[10]

We are familiar with how the Jewish apostle Saul chooses to go by his Roman name, Paul, not because of his conversion but because he pivots as the gospel moves from more Jewish territories into more obviously Roman settings (Acts 13:7–9). Something similar applies to Silvanus, who's known by this Roman name in the letters (1–2 Thessalonians; 2 Cor. 1:19; 1 Pet. 5:12) and by his alternative name, Silas, throughout Acts.

Scholars generally agree about the structure of the letters. The chapters break in helpful places, although they can be subdivided into smaller thematic sections as shown in figure 1. These sections are sometimes further subdivided; at other times, there is merit in noting how consecutive sections build into bigger movements.

| 1 Thessalonians | | | | | | 2 Thessalonians | | |
|---|---|---|---|---|---|---|---|---|
| 1 | 2 | 3 | 4 | 5 | | 1 | 2 | 3 |

Figure 1    Thematic sections in Thessalonians

10 Everyone recognizes the category of the apostles appointed by Jesus, and many recognize that the term "apostle" can refer as well not to a formal office but generally to those sent out for ministry (such as a teacher or missionary). Some believers and scholars wonder if God ceased commissioning the narrowest, most formal position after the church was founded. But most would accept that the broader sense of teacher or missionary continues today, even if the label "apostle" is not widely used. So we must be cautious in expecting to copy *every* ministry and authority of the first-century apostles even as we see and celebrate that God still grants many such skills today. See, e.g., Clinton E. Arnold, *Ephesians*, ZECNT 10 (Grand Rapids, MI: Zondervan, 2010), 255–59; Paul W. Barnett, "Apostle," *DPL*[1] 45–50; Cynthia Long Westfall, "Apostle," *DPL*[2] 49–53; Andrew Wilson, "Apostle Apollos?," *JETS* 56, no. 2 (2013): 325–35. But such a discussion is beyond the purview of this book.

Also, the notation "1 Thess. 2:6/7" is unfortunate. The long Greek sentence (2:5–7a) is arranged such that "apostles" appears at 2:6 in some English translations (ESV, NASB, NIV) and at 2:7 in others (CSB, NRSV).

For the sake of orientation, I give some rudimentary descriptions of these sections. My wording focuses on content, recognizing that the purpose and placement of such content is discussed in coming pages.

1 Thessalonians

| | |
|---|---|
| 1:1–10 | Thanksgiving for the believers and their conversion |
| 2:1–16 | Recollection of the apostles' loving ministry |
| 2:17–3:13 | Longing and prayers for visits and further growth |
| 4:1–12 | Detailed instructions for ongoing holy conduct |
| 4:13–18 | Assurance about dead believers at Jesus's return |
| 5:1–11 | Living in light of Jesus's time-unknown return |
| 5:12–28 | Succinct instructions for Christian conduct |

2 Thessalonians

| | |
|---|---|
| 1:1–12 | Thanksgiving for the believers and their endurance |
| 2:1–12 | Assurance that final judgment has not yet arrived |
| 2:13–17 | Further assurances, instructions, and prayers |
| 3:1–5 | Yet further assurances concerning perseverance |
| 3:6–18 | Instructions to deal with nonworking disruptors |

## A Relevant Church

So we start exploring letters directed to a church in good standing with its founders. Here is a young church whose planters are keen to give guidance on how believers can persevere and mature into seasoned veterans.

It is also a church whose social context is surprisingly similar to many in the twenty-first century. It faces overt and covert temptations to tone down its beliefs. It is largely Gentile and needs instruction via familiar, new covenant categories, even if these allude to whole-Bible concepts. Whether because its members suffer tender consciences or its leaders employ wise rhetoric (or both), these instructions come more as persistently gentle cajoling than aggressive confrontation. As David Williams identifies,

These letters were addressed to a small church in a large and overwhelmingly pagan society, a church under constant pressure to conform to the norms of that society. Many today can identify with the Thessalonians in this situation and can learn from Paul's sustained call to holiness that overcoming the pressure to conform demands consecration, not complacency.[11]

God willing, we are excited by these canonical letters for praising and encouraging a church progressing well. While the congregation is imperfect, it is refreshing to discover a series of largely positive examples we might imitate when walking through and pastoring every stage of the Christian journey.

---

11  David J. Williams, *1 and 2 Thessalonians*, NIBCNT 12 (Peabody, MA: Hendrickson, 1992), 16.

# 1

# You Turned to God

## Salvation and the Start of the Christian Journey

THE THESSALONIAN CORRESPONDENCE is devoted to cheering on fledgling believers. This is partly accomplished by fixing their eyes on the end of the course (cf. Phil. 3:12–14; Heb. 12:1–2), a strategy we investigate later (see chap. 3). But they also nourish confidence to complete the journey by repeatedly referencing the strong start already made.

### Biblical Images of Salvation

The Bible offers a surprising variety of metaphors for Christian salvation from peril: redeemed from slavery to serve a better master, reconciled or adopted into a family, judicially justified for a fresh lifestyle, reborn or transformed into a new person, brought from stumbling in darkness to walk in light, awarded a heavenly citizenship or inheritance, granted privileged access into God's secure presence, and so on. These images are often studied separately, so it's pleasing to see a growing number of resources that collate them and showcase their diversity.[1]

---

1 For a more popular-level treatment, see Victor Kuligin, *The Language of Salvation: Discovering the Riches of What It Means to Be Saved* (Bellingham, WA: Lexham, 2015); for a more scholarly volume, see Brenda B. Colijn, *Images of Salvation in the New Testament* (Downers Grove, IL: IVP Academic, 2010). Other substantial surveys include Michael F. Bird, *Evangelical Theology: A Biblical and Systematic Introduction*, 2nd ed. (Grand Rapids, MI: Zondervan Academic, 2020), 603–36; Douglas J. Moo, *A Theology of Paul and*

Most believers and preachers harbor one or two favorite models of salvation and think not to budge. We are sometimes ignorant of the breadth of the array. Paul, Silvanus, and Timothy publicize something of this variety in their letters.

I have chosen to shape this book under the rubric of a journey—more protracted than a race and more mundane than a pilgrimage—even though the image isn't drawn directly from the Thessalonian writings. This metaphor foregrounds valuable theological elements. It allows us to draw attention to the commencement of the journey; such commencement is sometimes the substantial or sole focus of scholarly and popular discussions of salvation. But the journey metaphor also recognizes a goal or an end point. And it acknowledges the effort required between start and finish to persevere against troublesome opponents and arduous circumstances. It invites questions about how to conduct and sustain oneself along the way. And it raises the possibility that not everyone who boldly ventures forth will necessarily complete the course. It is a thoroughly biblical metaphor, one that can be complemented with images of athletic contests and other competitive quests.[2]

## Thessalonian Images of Salvation

A quick catalogue of our letters' metaphors is valuable. Singling these out might protect us from skating too superficially or too uniformly over familiar terminology.

### Salvation

Five times the letters use overt language of "salvation" or "being saved," and once they mention spiritual "rescue." The two clearest examples accord well with contemporary Christian usage:

---

His Letters: The Gift of the New Realm in Christ, BTNT (Grand Rapids, MI: Zondervan Academic, 2021), 459–507, esp. 469–506.

2   Journey and athletic imagery is surprisingly underrepresented in most works cited in the prior footnote. For more consistent application of such imagery, see, e.g., Thomas R. Schreiner and Ardel B. Caneday, The Race Set before Us: A Biblical Theology of Perseverance and Assurance (Downers Grove, IL: IVP Academic, 2001).

> God has not destined us for wrath, but to obtain salvation through our Lord Jesus Christ. (1 Thess. 5:9)

> God chose you as the firstfruits to be saved, through sanctification by the Spirit and belief in the truth. (2 Thess. 2:13)

Both excerpts introduce additional language unpacked below. We also already glimpse all three persons of the Trinity participating in humanity's salvation. And the contexts of these examples accent how Thessalonian "salvation" is understood particularly as reprieve from God's final wrath.

Of course, we know to look for other terms, illustrating Christians' longstanding reliance on wider imagery of salvation.

### A Message Communicated and Received

Although it may appear obvious to the point of condescension, the Thessalonian letters are among those that most clearly demonstrate how images of salvation are packaged in words. The Christian gospel is a message communicated from one group of humans to another, using everyday conduits such as speaking and hearing or writing and reading. The following examples are transparent:

> We *proclaimed* to you the *gospel* of God. (1 Thess. 2:9; cf. 2:2)

> When you *received* the *word* of God, which you *heard* from us, you *accepted* it not as a human *word*, but as it actually is, the *word* of God. (1 Thess. 2:13 NIV)

> I put you under oath before the Lord to have this *letter read* to all. (1 Thess. 5:27)

> So then, brothers [and sisters],[3] stand firm and hold to the *traditions* that you were *taught* by us, either by our *spoken word* or by our *letter*. (2 Thess. 2:15; cf. 2:2; 3:6, 14)

---

3    I follow the ESV mg. notes in often clarifying "brothers *and sisters*" (cf. CSB, NASB 2020, NIV, NRSV). See, e.g., the ESV mg. notes on 1 Thess. 1:4 and 2 Thess. 1:3.

Such is the apostles' regular missionary quest, and they describe more broadly their *"speaking* to the Gentiles that they might be *saved"* (1 Thess. 2:16).

This brief selection hints at the prominence of "gospel" language; proportionally, only Galatians and Philippians use the term more densely. As with Paul's other writings, Thessalonians doesn't directly spell out what constitutes this good news; we're left to glean that from the wider theology of the letters. (Even "gospel"-saturated Galatians outlines the message more indirectly than directly. The passages in Rom. 1:1–4; 1 Cor. 15:1–11; and 2 Tim. 2:8 come closest to providing definitive content.) We need to continue our survey of Thessalonian images of salvation for insights into gospel content.[4]

The opening chapter introduces the two key descriptors: "Our *gospel* came to you," and "You received the *word"* (1 Thess. 1:5–6). These two nouns are regularly treated synonymously, and they're elsewhere linked together and with salvation (esp. 1 Cor. 15:1–2; Eph. 1:13). Something of their source and content is foreshadowed, especially once we realize that the connecting "of" is notoriously slippery both in English and in the Greek construction it renders. Consider the phrase "the songs *of* Michael Jackson." These are variously the songs performed by, composed by, owned by, or written about him.[5] In our letters, commentators are largely consistent in treating "the gospel/word of God" as being *from* God (1 Thess. 2:2, 8, 9, 13 [2x]) and "the word/gospel of the Lord / Lord Jesus / Christ" as being *about* Christ (1:8; 3:2; 4:15; 2 Thess. 1:8; 3:1).[6] The asymmetry may feel curious, and we should recognize that (1) it is usually and rightly the biblical context that helps us decide, (2) there is

---

4 On "gospel" in Paul, see Moo, *Theology of Paul,* 349–53, reprising Moo, *The Epistle to the Romans,* 2nd ed., NICNT (Grand Rapids, MI: Eerdmans, 2018), 54–58. His closing pages attempt a summary of Paul's gospel content.

5 I flesh out this illustration a little further, with examples, in Andrew Malone, *Knowing Jesus in the Old Testament? A Fresh Look at Christophanies* (Nottingham, UK: Inter-Varsity Press, 2015), 98.

6 These prepositions are helpfully clear in the translations and explications of Andy Johnson, *1 and 2 Thessalonians,* THNTC (Grand Rapids, MI: Eerdmans, 2016), 38, 50, 57, 60, 72, 73, 85, 86, 163, 206, 208.

more unanimity about "the *gospel* of God / the Lord" than about "the *word* of God / the Lord," and (3) these first two points explain why 1 Thessalonians 4:15 bucks the trend, with scholars in general accord with the ESV's phrasing: "a word *from* the Lord."[7]

As we continue developing a composite image of the gospel message, we can delight in its power (cf. Rom. 1:16; 1 Cor. 1:18). It is active like an additional participant in God's mission.[8] The same opening chapter rejoices that the word from God about Jesus is attended with power: the convicting work of the Holy Spirit (1 Thess. 1:5–6). The gospel continues to "work" among the Thessalonian believers (2:13), just as other biblical uses of this verb celebrate the energizing actions of God himself.[9] In one of the few prayers the missionaries request for themselves, they ask that this gospel message "speed ahead" further or faster in the world (2 Thess. 3:1; cf. Eph. 6:19–20). As Gary Shogren notes, "The gospel is not a series of philosophical chats, but a message through which the King himself changes lives."[10]

## Faith/Belief

The Thessalonian letters include a few mentions of the human element of "believing" the gospel message. Greek uses a single word group that's expressed by a variety of English terms concerning "belief" and "faith."

The believers' (!) faith is assumed in various passages (1 Thess. 1:3, 8; 3:2, 5, 6, 7, 10; 5:8; 2 Thess. 1:3–4, 11), and indeed, "believers" is one common shorthand for the faithful (!) in Thessalonica and elsewhere (1 Thess. 1:7; 2:10, 13; 2 Thess. 1:10). The object of such belief/faith

---

7   Note the dissent of Johnson, *1 and 2 Thessalonians*, 126–27. When elsewhere the phrase connotes "a word *about* the Lord," Johnson sees no warrant here to explore some fresh or unrecorded message *from* the Lord Jesus.

8   Patrick Schreiner, *The Mission of the Triune God: A Theology of Acts*, NTT (Wheaton, IL: Crossway, 2022), 79–81.

9   See the tidy list in Gene L. Green, *The Letters to the Thessalonians*, PNTC (Grand Rapids, MI: Eerdmans, 2002), 140. Note the CSB's stronger translation: "works effectively."

10   Gary S. Shogren, *1 & 2 Thessalonians*, ZECNT 13 (Grand Rapids, MI: Zondervan, 2012), 109; cf. Green, *Thessalonians*, 141.

is also clarified. As we might expect, salvation involves "faith *in God*," including the doctrinal confession of Jesus's death and resurrection (1 Thess. 1:8; 4:14). The alternative to believing such truth is to believe falsehood (2 Thess. 2:11–13). The language of believing a message or truth is sometimes extended to "receiving," "accepting," "welcoming," or even "loving" it (1 Thess. 1:6; 2:13 [2x]; 4:1; 2 Thess. 2:10; 3:6). Thus, even though "faith" is sometimes linked with "hope" and "love" (1 Thess. 1:3; 5:8; cf. 1 Cor. 13:13), one analyst fairly argues that it's faith that portrays "the essential response to the gospel."[11]

We must not, however, overprioritize faith or mischaracterize it. In coming chapters we see that the Thessalonian letters also praise love and hope as essential results of embracing the gospel. And modern studies continue the Reformation tradition that saving belief is not merely cerebral cognition; it also involves willing assent and ongoing, obedient trust.[12] Thessalonians is as much concerned with persistent "faithfulness" as with an initial declaration of "faith."[13]

## A New Family

Perhaps the dominant description of the Thessalonians who have believed and been saved is familial. Just as the church planters describe themselves in family terms (see chap. 4), so too they describe their Christian flock as "brothers [and sisters]" (1 Thess. 1:4; 2:1, 9, 14, 17; 3:7; 4:1, 6, 10 [2x], 13; 5:1, 4, 12, 14, 25, 26, 27; 2 Thess. 1:3; 2:1, 13, 15; 3:1, 6 [2x], 13, 15). Of course, dozens of occurrences appear throughout the Pauline corpus.

11  Allan Chapple, "Paul's Ministry of the Word according to 1 Thessalonians," in *Serving God's Words: Windows on Preaching and Ministry*, ed. Paul A. Barker, Richard J. Condie, and Andrew S. Malone (Nottingham, UK: Inter-Varsity Press, 2011), 90–91.
12  Michael S. Horton presents a wide-ranging yet compact summary of these elements (*notitia, assensus, fiducia*) in *The Christian Faith: A Systematic Theology for Pilgrims on the Way* (Grand Rapids, MI: Zondervan, 2011), 582–83.
13  See the helpful summaries and sources of Nijay K. Gupta, *1 & 2 Thessalonians*, ZCINT 13 (Grand Rapids, MI: Zondervan Academic, 2019), 61, 93–95; elaborated in Gupta, *Paul and the Language of Faith* (Grand Rapids, MI: Eerdmans, 2020). Cf. Matthew W. Bates, *Salvation by Allegiance Alone: Rethinking Faith, Works, and the Gospel of Jesus the King* (Grand Rapids, MI: Baker Academic, 2017).

As with other images of salvation, this language may be so familiar that we neither notice its prevalence nor appreciate its cultural
relevance in New Testament times. I have provided an exhaustive list
to underscore the ubiquity. Building on this frequency, Trevor Burke
demonstrates the Pauline strategy of creating and repeatedly reinforcing
new church-family identities for Christian converts.[14] This prominent
family imagery is an attractive invitation for believers and unbelievers,
past and present, whose own families have been fractured.

## Additional Images

Several other metaphors make cameo appearances, although in no
sustained way. These confirm both that the authors maintain a broad
arsenal of imagery and that these are consistent with—and often further
developed in—later New Testament writings.

The language of day and light is contrasted with night and darkness in 1 Thessalonians 5:4–8, clearly demarcating those who em-
brace the gospel message from those who reject it. Such imagery is
found throughout the Old Testament (e.g., Prov. 4:18–19; Isa. 8:20–9:2;
59:9–10) and other ancient cultures. The Johannine writings especially
favor this contrast (e.g., John 1:4–9; 3:19–21; 11:9–10; 12:35–36; 1 John
1:5–7; 2:8–11; Rev. 21:22–22:5). Of course, the imagery can be found
elsewhere (e.g., Matt. 5:14–16; 6:22–23; Luke 1:79; 16:8; 1 Pet. 2:9),
including in Paul's later letters (Rom. 13:12–13; 2 Cor. 4:3–6; Eph.
5:8–14; Col. 1:12–13). Our own contemporary fiction and nonfiction
accounts maintain such traditions of "the forces of light" versus "the
dark side."

Akin to the contrast between light and darkness, salvation in the
New Testament is as much about salvation *for* as salvation *from*. Believers are freed from slavery to sin to become enslaved to righteousness

---

14  Trevor J. Burke, "Mother, Father, Infant, Orphan, Brother: Paul's Variegated Pastoral
Strategy towards His Thessalonian Church Family," in *Paul as Pastor*, ed. Brian S. Rosner,
Andrew S. Malone, and Trevor J. Burke (London: Bloomsbury T&T Clark, 2018), e.g.,
126–27, 137–41. From the "staggering" number of references, he judges that "Thessalonians breathes brotherly/sisterly language" (126).

and to God (Rom. 6:15–23; 1 Pet. 2:24). We escape the fearful powers of evil and enter the security of God's presence (2 Tim. 4:16–18; Heb. 2:14–18). We have emigrated from death to life (John 5:21–26; Rom. 4:17; 6:1–4; Eph. 2:5; 1 John 3:14). Old earthly passions are replaced with new heavenly priorities (e.g., Col. 3:1–14; cf. 2 Cor. 5:17; 2 Tim. 1:9–10). The change of allegiance in 1 Thessalonians 1:9 gives the inspiration for this chapter's title: "You turned to God from idols to serve the living and true God." Our next chapter explores what this new service looks like.

## Absent Images

Although it's not my quest to list all the salvific images that Thessalonians *fails* to employ, it does us good to acknowledge that these letters are not Mark or Philippians or our other favored writings. As with most Pauline letters, each of the Thessalonian epistles contains only one mention of God's "kingdom" (1 Thess. 2:12; 2 Thess. 1:5). So the Thessalonian pair is not the Gospels or 1 Corinthians. The behavior of the missionaries and the conduct of God are each praised once as "righteous/just" (1 Thess. 2:10; 2 Thess. 1:5–6), but there's no further linguistic whiff of the "righteousness/justification" that much discussion of Pauline theology focuses on. So Thessalonians isn't Romans or Galatians. Conversely, Thessalonians does include two additional metaphors that *are* sufficiently prominent to warrant separate headings.

## The Value of Holiness

While Thessalonians says little about justification, at least using that language, it makes more frequent mention of sanctification and holiness. (Just as English uses "faith" and "belief" for a concentrated Greek concept, so "sanctification" and "holiness" are varied English ways of describing a single Greek idea.) The matter is sufficiently central that it requires thoughtful inspection.

Some church traditions have overly segregated the language of justification and sanctification, as if the former is only an initial change in status before God and the latter purely God's subsequent work in believers. The corresponding biblical terms do not always align with the helpful systematic categories. Careful interpreters observe that "being sanctified" can equally describe the *initial* work and might often be better communicated with a phrase like "being pronounced holy." Like justification, this is a change in positional status before God. Various passages even correlate "righteousness/justification" with "sanctification" (esp. 1 Cor. 1:30; 6:11).[15] David Peterson is a leading proponent of this view, arguing that a significant proportion of the Bible's "sanctification" language carries this positional or definitive sense. His preferred terminology connects regeneration, justification, *and* sanctification as descriptions of initial conversion, which is subsequently followed by progressive renewal, transformation, and growth.[16]

Thessalonians certainly speaks about progressive renewal and growth. But much of its language of "sanctification" concerns initial conversion, using this terminology rather than "justification." The flagship verse is 2 Thessalonians 2:13, which rejoices "because God chose you . . . to be saved, through sanctification by the Spirit and belief in the truth."

In turn, as throughout the New Testament letters, believing Christians are described as "the holy ones" or "the saints/sanctified" (2 Thess. 1:10; perhaps 1 Thess. 3:13).[17] The passage in 2 Thessalonians 1:10 makes the point especially clearly:

---

15  Thomas R. Schreiner, *Paul, Apostle of God's Glory in Christ: A Pauline Theology*, 2nd ed. (Downers Grove, IL: IVP Academic, 2020), 235–38.

16  David G. Peterson, *Possessed by God: A New Testament Theology of Sanctification and Holiness*, NSBT 1 (Leicester, UK: Apollos, 1995); summarized in Peterson, "Holiness," in *NDBT* 544–50.

17  Despite most major translations reading "saints," a growing number of commentators insist that 1 Thess. 3:13 describes God's "holy *angels*" attending Jesus at his return. Confident proponents include Green, *Thessalonians*, 181; Gordon D. Fee, *The First and Second Letters to the Thessalonians*, NICNT (Grand Rapids, MI: Eerdmans, 2009), 135–36. One representative of those favoring "holy *people*" (i.e., believers) is Jeffrey A. D. Weima, *1–2 Thessalonians*, BECNT 13 (Grand Rapids, MI: Baker Academic, 2014), 242–43. All commentators acknowledge that the language of "holy ones" *could* describe human believers and that it regularly does elsewhere.

. . . when he comes to be glorified *among his holy people*
and to be marveled at *among all who have believed.* (my trans.)

My own translation here displays the close parallelism I'm promoting throughout our survey: that "believing" and "being sanctified /
pronounced holy" describe the same group of people at the same
point in time. "Sanctification" in Thessalonians does not apply only to
subsequent transformation.

One final passage identifies the prominence of holiness in
Thessalonians:

For this is the will of God, your *sanctification.* . . . For God has not
called us for impurity, but in *holiness.* Therefore whoever disregards
this, disregards not man but God, who gives his Holy Spirit to you.
(1 Thess. 4:3, 7–8)

These verses frame an important passage about holy living, which we
explore in the next chapter. The frame repeats the same key term, and the
ESV demonstrates how "sanctification" and "holiness" are interchange-
able English renderings. God has called believers to a God-worthy status
of holiness, and only thence might we speak *also* of additional sanctification. "Holiness" describes a state of being "God-worthy"—suitable for his
reputation and presence—and it is only a secondary and derivative step to
apply it to pious behavior. Nor is it any accident that this passage includes
the related adjective for the person of the Godhead who brings God's
empowering presence among his sanctified people: God's *Holy* Spirit.

The passage helps us grasp the potential confusion in theological
and church conversations. God has declared his people holy, and so
they need to get on with living up to the family standard. It's a story we
know well from family dynasties in political or business or community
life: the family line has a reputation, a name for itself, which its heirs
are expected to uphold. This is the persistent cry of Thessalonians and
the rest of the New Testament:

We exhorted each one of you and encouraged you and charged you to walk in a manner worthy of God. (1 Thess. 2:12; cf. 4:1)

To this end we always pray for you, that our God may make you worthy of his calling. (2 Thess. 1:11)

I . . . urge you to walk in a manner worthy of the calling to which you have been called. (Eph. 4:1; cf. Phil. 1:27; Col. 1:9–10)

Bear fruit in keeping with repentance. (Matt. 3:8; cf. Luke 3:8; James 2:14–26)

Michael Horton captures the sense emphatically: "*Where most people think that the goal of religion is to get people to become something that they are not, the Scriptures call believers to become more and more what they already are in Christ.*"[18] The Bible's language of holiness and sanctification is key to this call.

## A Confident Calling

Already we have seen several verses connected with salvation that refer to God's "calling" or "choosing" of the Thessalonian believers. This launches us into the murky waters of election and predestination, where some of us (myself included) fear to wade. But the language pervades these letters and invites us to explore the topic. Further examples reinforce its prominence:

For we know, brothers [and sisters] loved by God, that he has *chosen* you. (1 Thess. 1:4)

For God has not *destined* us for wrath, but to obtain salvation through our Lord Jesus Christ. (1 Thess. 5:9)

---

18  Horton, *Christian Faith*, 652 (emphasis original).

God . . . *calls* you into his own kingdom and glory. (1 Thess. 2:12; cf. 4:7; 5:24; 2 Thess. 1:11; 2:13–14)

The apostles' presupposition of God's election can be expressed or assumed without these exact words. Counting even a limited choice of terms or concepts, we find the Thessalonian letters more densely concerned with this issue than any other Pauline writing—and 2 Thessalonians more invested than 1 Thessalonians.[19]

### Theological Factors

Theological discussions of election, especially in Paul's writings, can orbit three issues. How do divine and human wills coincide? Does God direct only the fates of whole groups, or does election extend to specific individuals? And if God elects some for salvation, can we talk about him electing others for the opposite?

Those seeking a tidy, logical resolution to the first topic face disappointment. The interplay between divine and human actions working for salvation remains heavily discussed because the Bible speaks confidently of both.[20] Thessalonians likewise articulates both, often in the same breath. Many read 1 Thessalonians 5:9 to say that *God* actively destined us that *we* might actively obtain salvation (cf. Acts 16:14; Phil. 2:12–13). Multiple responsibilities are interwoven throughout 2 Thessalonians 2:13–15, which we can adapt and stylize like this:

*God* chose you . . . to be saved,
    through sanctification by the *Spirit*
    and [through *your*] belief in the truth.

---

19  The exhaustive survey remains I. Howard Marshall, "Election and Calling to Salvation in 1 and 2 Thessalonians," in *The Thessalonian Correspondence*, ed. Raymond F. Collins, BETL 87 (Leuven, Belgium: Leuven University Press, 1990), 259–76. One notable "trade-off" is that there are only two mentions of "grace" (2 Thess. 1:12; 2:16) outside the letters' formulaic bookends (1 Thess. 1:1; 5:28; 2 Thess. 1:2; 3:16, 18)—and even those occurrences fall in closing summaries. Divine "peace" is similarly marginalized. And Thessalonians makes no mention of "mercy" of any sort.

20  J. I. Packer, *Evangelism and the Sovereignty of God* (1961; repr., Downers Grove, IL: IVP Books, 2012), e.g., 27–29.

To this *he* called you
>   through *our* gospel,
>   so that *you* may obtain
>       the glory of our Lord Jesus Christ.
> So then, brothers [and sisters], [*you* must] stand firm
>   and hold to the traditions that you were taught by *us*.

We see the human responsibilities of speakers as much as of hearers.[21] We comprehend why Thessalonian scholars readily recognize both divine and human activity—and why scholars and pastors continue to explore the biblical balance between them.

The second election issue concerns groups versus individuals. The language of God's choice is especially familiar from Romans (Rom. 8:33; 9:11; 11:5, 7, 28; 16:13). Election there is indeed *phrased* along group boundaries: God's plans for Jews and Gentiles. But this still necessitates *applying* election to some individuals and not others.[22]

Our Thessalonian letters contribute lightly in this same direction. Most Christian believers in Thessalonica hailed from a Gentile background (Acts 17:1–4; 1 Thess. 1:9)—so much so that Acts can immediately use "the Jews" to label those not persuaded by Paul's synagogue discourses (Acts 17:5). Thessalonians thus corroborates Romans 9 that God's election boundaries can be (1) narrowed to some Jews and not all and (2) widened to include some Gentiles.[23] Implicit is God's free choice of individuals, unconstrained by their ethnic or religious heritage. And we find no relevant corporate language, such as "chosen/called *in Christ*" (cf. Eph. 1:4), on which some rely for the alternate view favoring corporate election.

---

21 For divine predestination of *preachers*, see, e.g., Jer. 20:7–9; Amos 3:7–8; Acts 4:18–20; Rom. 1:14–15; 1 Cor. 9:16–17; 2 Cor. 5:18–20.

22 Moo, *Romans*, 589, 591–92, 605–7, 692–93, 752–53. Witherington is one who insists that the language of election applies only to groups, even in Thessalonians. Ben Witherington III, *The Letters to Philemon, the Colossians, and the Ephesians: A Socio-Rhetorical Commentary on the Captivity Epistles* (Grand Rapids, MI: Eerdmans, 2007), 233–35; Witherington, *1 and 2 Thessalonians: A Socio-Rhetorical Commentary* (Grand Rapids, MI: Eerdmans, 2006), 65.

23 Moo, *Romans*, 589.

As in most other letters, the collective Thessalonian church is addressed. So it can be fairly objected that God has called the entire assembly. Yet there are glimpses of the individuals composing the group. The apostles have not burdened "any [one] of you" (1 Thess. 2:9; 2 Thess. 3:8). Individual Thessalonian believers should not misbehave (1 Thess. 5:15; 2 Thess. 3:6, 10, 14–15). We hear examples and instructions concerning the encouragement of "each one" of the church's members (1 Thess. 2:11–12; 3:3; 4:4; 5:11; 2 Thess. 1:3). Taken together, these points probably lend support to the notion of individual election.

The third election debate is both intellectually and emotionally vexing. Assuming God positively elects some people to salvation, what might we say about God's treatment of others?

Many systematic theologians and Pauline scholars are reluctant to frame God as proactively condemning nonelect sinners, an activity sometimes labeled "double predestination." Pauline passages often say little about God's responsibility for those not actively chosen for salvation.[24] Systematicians likewise highlight asymmetries: reprobation is not the negative mirror of election. Millard Erickson is especially valuable in spotlighting the subtle difference in God's inaction in the demise of nonelect sinners. Such approaches accentuate fallen human choices.[25]

Other Pauline and systematic theologians give full weight to God's proactivity: Thomas Schreiner argues, "He chooses to have mercy on some, and he chooses to harden others."[26] Michael Bird confesses that God's sovereign purposes include "reprobation in

---

24   On Eph. 1:4, see, e.g., Lynn H. Cohick, *The Letter to the Ephesians*, NICNT (Grand Rapids, MI: Eerdmans, 2020), 95 and references therein. On Rom. 9:22–23, see Moo, *Romans*, 618–19; cf. Moo, *Theology of Paul*, 530n47.

25   Millard J. Erickson, *Christian Theology*, 3rd ed. (Grand Rapids, MI: Baker Academic, 2013), 319, 850–51; Wayne A. Grudem, *Systematic Theology: An Introduction to Biblical Doctrine*, 2nd ed. (Grand Rapids, MI: Zondervan Academic, 2020), 817, 835–36; Horton, *Christian Faith*, 317.

26   Thomas R. Schreiner, *Romans*, 2nd ed., BECNT (Grand Rapids, MI: Baker Academic, 2018), 494; cf. 499–500, 509–10. He elsewhere bluntly outlines God assigning and being the ultimate cause of "both salvation and perdition." *Paul*, 263.

judgment."[27] Perhaps most famous is John Calvin, who, alongside many similar comments, insists that "God adopts some to hope of life, and sentences others to eternal death."[28]

The Thessalonian letters testify to multiple parties' involvement in human unbelief:

- Unbelievers are described as personally culpable. They don't know God or obey the gospel or welcome its truth but prefer unrighteousness or wickedness (2 Thess. 1:8; 2:10–12). They act badly toward God's people and others and thus displease him (1 Thess. 2:15–16; 2 Thess. 1:6).

- Forces of evil are named—Satan, the tempter, the evil one, the enigmatic "man of lawlessness"—as is something of their "power and false signs and wonders" and their "wicked deception for those who are perishing" (1 Thess. 2:18; 3:5; 2 Thess. 2:3–12; 3:3; quotations from 2 Thess. 2:3, 9–10). As with positive examples of divine and human wills coinciding for salvation, so we hear of demonic and human wills colluding for disobedience.

- Such actions are not outside God's oversight. Consider Job (Job 1:6–12; 2:1–7), Paul's thorn in the flesh (2 Cor. 12:7–9), and Jesus's brutal crucifixion. Evil actions of Satan and humans are foreknown and tolerated by God and accord with his "will" or "plan" (esp. Acts 2:23; 4:27–28). Our letters certainly show God rescuing some people and leaving others to wrathful judgment (1 Thess. 1:4–10). Yet the letters also cast him as more active. As Satan works false signs and wonders to deceive those refusing to love the truth, God works in concert as well (2 Thess. 2:9–12): "God sends them a strong delusion, *so that* they may believe what is false, *in order that* all may be condemned who did not believe the truth but had pleasure in unrighteousness" (2:11–12).

27  Bird, *Evangelical Theology*, 570. He assesses election and its pastoral application positively in Bird, *Romans*, SGBC 6 (Grand Rapids, MI: Zondervan, 2016), 336–43.

28  John Calvin, *Institutes of the Christian Religion* (1559), ed. John T. McNeill, trans. Ford Lewis Battles, 2 vols., LCC 20–21 (Philadelphia: Westminster, 1960), 2:926 (3.21.5).

This language from 2 Thessalonians 2:11–12 is among the Bible's strongest claims to God's direct involvement in sinners' demise. Some interpreters take comfort that this sentence opens with "for this reason" (ESV: "therefore"): God's dispatching of a delusion *responds* to human decisions already made. Although this reality softens God's culpability, it threatens to excuse him from the driver's seat and surrender his control to human choices under the influence of evil. Thessalonians gives a balanced view of each party's participation. This includes due weight given to God's active involvement in blinding—and in letting Satan blind—those not welcoming the message of salvation (cf. Rom. 9:14–29; 11:7–8; 2 Cor. 4:3–4; Rev. 13:1–4, 11–15).[29]

## Pastoral Corollaries

One danger in discussing calling and election and predestination is that, intentionally or inadvertently, we might "mislocate" ourselves and thus misapply the doctrines. Our apostles model responsible ways forward.

We might mislocate our authority to judge an individual's or group's status. The Thessalonian letters have much to say about *God's* judgment. The apostles anticipate the verdicts they expect God to pronounce, based on the visible fruit of those currently working for or against God's kingdom (e.g., 1 Thess. 1:2–10; 2:13–16; 5:4–8; 2 Thess. 1:3–8). But they acknowledge the limitations of their estimates. Despite confidence in the Thessalonians' initial reception of the gospel, they desperately seek confirmation that the new believers are continuing to take root and grow (1 Thess. 3:1–5).

They seek this evidence because the apostles do not mislocate themselves in time. Election and salvation are validated only at journey's end. A runner may start well, but we know her record-breaking time—and that she will even complete the course—only once she crosses the finish line (cf. Phil. 3:12–14). In Jesus's parable, three of the four soils

---

29  Longer discussions of election within the context of Thessalonian commentaries, showcasing varying perspectives, include Shogren, *1 & 2 Thessalonians*, 307–12; Witherington, *1 and 2 Thessalonians*, 65–70; cf. Johnson, *1 and 2 Thessalonians*, 316–29.

sprout promising seedlings; *at that point*, we do not know which one will flourish for harvest (Luke 8:4–15).

As a race progresses or a crop ripens, confidence in the outcome builds. Our authors are buoyed by how the Thessalonians have begun their course and how they're advancing. We witness increasingly excited coaches, cheering on their charges as the prize draws closer and looks ever more certain—and as pressure threatens to sap perseverance. The apostles model the encouragement they command the Thessalonians to offer each other (1 Thess. 4:18; 5:11). This accords well with other biblical calls to encourage and confirm election and to stave off fatigue (e.g., 2 Cor. 13:5–6; Heb. 3:1–6, 12–14; 2 Pet. 1:10–11; 2 John 8; Rev. 2:25–26).

This is the pastoral purpose for which divine election is articulated, a point all biblical interpreters agree on. It is positive encouragement along the way rather than a premature declaration of success (or of failure). The apostles recall evidence that God "chose" the Thessalonian believers to start their journey (1 Thess. 1:4; 2 Thess. 2:13–14). They attest to God's ongoing work among them (1 Thess. 3:6–8). Thus they pray for endurance, confident from a human perspective that the Thessalonians are among those whom God will persevere through final judgment (1 Thess. 3:12–13; 5:23–24; 2 Thess. 1:11–12).

## Images of Ongoing Salvation

The Bible presents three "tenses" of salvation: what God has completed, what he is still working at, and what he will one day finalize. "*Salvation*, in other words," Thomas Schreiner and Ardel Caneday clarify, "is not only a term to describe what God has already done by justifying and converting us but also a word that portrays what God has not yet done when he will bring us to 'the goal of our faith, the salvation of our souls' (1 Pet 1.9)."[30] Thessalonians not only outlines its commencement and goal but also stirs us to think about God's *current* transformation of believers.

---

30  Schreiner and Caneday, *Race Set before Us*, 43–44.

Our next chapter considers what this transformation effects in our behaviors. But the present discussion of salvation invites mention of God's
ongoing renovation. Notice the "right now" language of key verses:

> Walk in a manner worthy of God, who *[continually] calls* you into
> his own kingdom and glory . . . [partly by means of] the word of
> God, which *is [now] at work* in you believers. (1 Thess. 2:12–13)

> Now may the God of peace himself sanctify you completely. . . .
> He who *[continually] calls* you is faithful; he will surely do it.
> (1 Thess. 5:23–24)

Of course, this reminds us of other passages in which believers remain
God's works in progress (e.g., Phil. 1:6).

The present tense (as well as the future tense) applies to a number
of our salvation terms. The quote above from 1 Thessalonians 5:23–24
shows that the "sanctification" already declared of believers continues
to transform them. Among God's actions, positional sanctification
leads to progressive renewal. Among our responses, initial declarations
of "faith" lead to ongoing "faithfulness." The Thessalonian letters are
again to the fore in such teaching. When Douglas Moo insists that "it is
vital to recognize that Paul views faith as fundamental to the Christian
life from beginning *to end*," he lists twenty-seven passages concerning
"continuing" faith and growth, a full third of which are from Thessalonians.[31] Focused investigation of the letters themselves confirms that,
in Paul Rainbow's words, "faith is not only a past, one-time response
to God's first call but also a present, ever renewed response to God's
calling until his kingdom arrives."[32]

The Thessalonian letters have introduced us to a range of images
describing the start of the Christian journey, images that complement

---

31   Moo, *Theology of Paul*, 529 (emphasis added). See also Schreiner, *Paul*, e.g., 60–61, 225–27,
     294–97.
32   Paul A. Rainbow, "Justification according to Paul's Thessalonian Correspondence," *BBR* 19
     (2009): 259.

the rest of Paul and the New Testament and that foreground the biblical theme of holiness. The members of "the church of the Thessalonians in God the Father and the Lord Jesus Christ" (1 Thess. 1:1; cf. 2 Thess. 1:1) have begun their journey admirably. We turn now to consider their next steps.

# 2

# To Walk and to Please God

Christian Living between Jesus's
First and Second Comings

THE THESSALONIAN LETTERS remind us that initial salvation is the beginning of an ongoing journey. Believers do not make a profession of faith, instantly find themselves cryogenically frozen, and then awaken for eternal life in the new heavens and new earth. Several threads from the prior chapter converge as we probe further how Christian believers should live before reaching their earthly journey's end.

## A Flourishing, Visible Holiness

Already we have to watch our "tenses" of salvation. Some churches speak of a "salvation prayer," and we certainly celebrate when a new believer responds to God's call. Yet this is but the first step in the Christian walk; believers continue to "grow up into salvation" (1 Pet. 2:1–3). We might say that initial conversion is just the first of many stages in God's ongoing transformation of a sin-marred human. C. S. Lewis concurs: "How little they know of Christianity who think that the story *ends* with conversion."[1]

---

1  C. S. Lewis, *The Collected Letters of C. S. Lewis*, ed. Walter Hooper, 3 vols. (2004–2007), 3:425.

The different tenses of salvation correlate with the different senses of sanctification and holiness. God's initial declaration of someone's holiness leads to an ongoing quest to conform to the family likeness and uphold the family reputation. As much as the letter of James or any other part of the Bible, Thessalonians is adamant that God's work of initial theological sanctification gives birth to a joint divine-human project of ongoing practical holiness. We have already seen Michael Horton's phrasing: "*The Scriptures call believers to become more and more what they already are in Christ.*"[2] Horton even subtitles his thousand-page study of Christian doctrine accordingly: *A Systematic Theology for Pilgrims on the Way.*

This theme of sanctification/holiness triangulates neatly with our study of God's calling and election. Believers are elected not merely *from* sin, nor only *for* salvation, but *for* the goal of being holy and blameless (Eph. 1:4). We see shortly that this idea, as expressed in one of the later Pauline letters, is found also among the earliest in 1 and 2 Thessalonians.

*Essential Fruit*

We recognize various Christian virtues. Faith, hope, and love are the most famous. We know them from the climax of Paul's chapter on love (1 Cor. 13:13) and from elsewhere in Scripture (most clearly Gal. 5:5–6; Col. 1:4–5). The triad appears also in Thessalonians (1 Thess. 1:3; 5:8). These virtues are always active. They are not ends in themselves; they produce fruit. And the fruitfulness of the famous threesome sparks the apostles' thanksgiving for their Thessalonian flock:

> We always thank God for all of you, [remembering] . . . your work *produced by* faith, your labor *motivated by* love, and your endurance *inspired by* hope in our Lord Jesus Christ. (1 Thess. 1:2–3 CSB; cf. NIV)

---

2   Michael S. Horton, *The Christian Faith: A Systematic Theology for Pilgrims on the Way* (Grand Rapids, MI: Zondervan, 2011), 652 (emphasis original).

Faith, love, and hope are visible in the Thessalonians' conduct. Much the same combination of virtues and resulting fruit anchor the opening thanksgiving of the second letter (2 Thess. 1:3–4). And it's the fruit, more than the virtues, for which God is praised.

The chain of fruitfulness is linked even more clearly in 2 Thessalonians 1:11. The apostles pray regularly that God would (1) "make you worthy of his calling" and (2) "bring to fruition your every desire for goodness and your every deed prompted by faith" (NIV). The first petition confirms that God continues to work in those whom he elects/calls. The second contains several elements, including another instance of God working alongside human desires—although here the apostles are so confident in the Thessalonians' resolutions that they simply ask God to fall in line with them! Again, the focus is on the practical outworking of obedient trust: "every deed prompted by faith" (NIV). A similar prayer in 2:16–17 likewise seeks to establish the Thessalonians "in every good work and word."

We turn to consider some of the more specific expressions of faith and other virtues. As we do so, it's worth recognizing that the apostles are praising deeds that are already moving in the right direction. They reinforce the Thessalonians' positive habits by thanking God for them—and by telling the Thessalonians of such thankfulness. They name what is going well even as they call for its repetition and increase. And we see again that faith and sanctification and their public outworking are expected to develop and flourish. There is no "resting on one's laurels" and little indication of a church investing the least passable effort. Nijay Gupta laments how "too many Christians (of every generation) have desired a kind of minimum-standard moral system to follow which often results in believers lining up as closely as possible to the boundary of sin, but just barely on the 'holy' side."[3] But here in Thessalonians we witness the promising signs of God's past and present transformation of believers that makes them increasingly "holy"—that is, increasingly suited to his reputation and to his presence both now and for eternity.

---

3   Nijay K. Gupta, *1–2 Thessalonians*, NCCS (Eugene, OR: Cascade, 2016), 80.

*Habitual Holiness*

The majority of the Thessalonian Christians give no impression of a minimalist holiness. They are not seeking a barely passing grade, dallying as close to the pleasures of sin as they might get away with. We return shortly to some of the apostles' most specific instructions for those we might call "boundary riders."

Rather, the Thessalonians mostly exhibit positive habits, and the apostles call them to be even more proactive in nurturing such habits. We see this in the letters' strongest calls to a holy lifestyle that is commensurate with their holy status:

> We exhorted each one of you and encouraged you and charged you to walk in a manner worthy of God, who calls you into his own kingdom and glory. (1 Thess. 2:12)

> We ask and urge you in the Lord Jesus, that as you received from us how you ought to walk and to please God, just as you are doing, that you do so more and more. . . . For this is the will of God, your sanctification. (1 Thess. 4:1, 3)

Such linked chains of fruitfulness should indeed sound familiar to us; they reoccur in some of Paul's later and often better-known letters. In Colossians 1:9–12, Paul and Timothy use much the same vocabulary to pray that believers might "*walk* in a manner *worthy* of the Lord, fully *pleasing* to him: *bearing fruit* in every *good work* and *increasing*" in God's knowledge, strength, and power, exhibiting all this fruitfulness in their endurance, patience, joy, and thanksgiving. A similar outworking and similar behaviors fill the latter half of Ephesians, all stemming from the pivotal instruction at Ephesians 4:1 that believers should "*walk* in a manner *worthy* of *the calling* to which [they] have *been called*."

The language of "walking" is valuable. It's clearly a metaphor for the regular conduct of one's life, not just one's gait. We readily recall related injunctions throughout the writings of Paul and John, echoing the equivalent Old Testament metaphor. Believers "walk not according to the flesh but according to the Spirit" (Rom. 8:4) and "keep in step with the Spirit" (Gal. 5:25; cf. 5:16). We are to "walk in the light" rather than "in darkness," walking as Jesus walked (1 John 1:6–7; cf. 2:6). There are many more images like these. It makes perfect sense that all English translations occasionally render the idiom as "to live" (most often the NIV), especially in Paul, where the verb is "always used metaphorically for a person's lifestyle."[4] We must renounce bad lifestyle habits and cultivate good lifestyle habits. And the outcome is to please God. Interpreters often see the apostolic commands here as meaning "to walk *so as* to please God."

## Detailed Instructions

The key command from 1 Thessalonians 4:1 directs the Thessalonians "to walk and to please God"—lifestyle expectations after which our current chapter (as well as this book) is titled. Just as Ephesians 4:1 pivots that letter from "theory" to "practice," so 1 Thessalonians 4:1 introduces an intense focus on holy living that fills the last two chapters with a series of instructions.[5]

We should note three recurrent elements in the introductory verses (4:1–2) and the two chapters. (1) The apostles are repeating instructions they had already given in person. When nurturing holy behavior, there is room for repetition. (2) The Thessalonians are already walking in the right direction. When nurturing holy behavior, there is room for positive reinforcement, not only correction of misbehavior. (3) The apostles suggest that there always remains room for further development, just as few athletes stop training each time they score a new personal best. Until we are fully sanctified for God's presence at the coming of our

---

4  Benjamin L. Merkle, *United to Christ, Walking in the Spirit: A Theology of Ephesians*, NTT (Wheaton, IL: Crossway, 2022), 74–75. Here Merkle starts a corresponding study of Paul's expectations of lifestyle behavior.

5  One accessible overview of 1 Thess. 4–5 is Gordon D. Fee, *The First and Second Letters to the Thessalonians*, NICNT (Grand Rapids, MI: Eerdmans, 2009), 136–37.

Lord Jesus Christ (5:23), nurturing holy behavior means that we aspire to "excel still more" (4:1 NASB 1995).[6]

We have also been tracking the balance between divine activity and human responsibility. It is insightful that as soon as the apostles pray to "supply what is lacking" in the Thessalonians' faith (3:10) and that the Lord Jesus would keep strengthening the Thessalonians to be "blameless in holiness" (3:13), they write with practical steps for the Thessalonians to obey. Both God and believers are accountable for believers' growth in faithful holiness.

*To Walk and to Please God—in Sexual Conduct*

The first detailed issue for which the Thessalonians need reminding and persistent excellence concerns sexual conduct. Some Bibles continue directly from 1 Thessalonians 4:1–2 into 4:3–8, but it's useful to consider the latter as a new paragraph (so CSB, NIV). We have already seen that this new paragraph is framed by attention to sanctification and holiness: four mentions in six verses (4:3–4, 7–8).

The day I first drafted these comments, the world's most populous Muslim nation formally criminalized all sex outside marriage. Much of the Western world reeled, aghast at this curtailment of sexual freedom. First-century Christians from Gentile backgrounds would have been equally surprised at the apostles' call for monogamous sex; their permissive society was little different from today's West.[7] The countercultural nature of this command to the Thessalonians may explain its prominent placement and length. Yes, the apostles had meant it when they taught in person, and they still mean it as they teach now via letter.

A complex sentence interweaves several expressions that ultimately explain each other. We can represent the core skeleton of 4:3–6 this way:

6   Rhetorical techniques like these are hardly new. Commentators often identify relevant ancient wisdom; see, e.g., Timothy A. Brookins, *First and Second Thessalonians*, Paideia (Grand Rapids, MI: Baker Academic, 2021), 82–83.

7   Commentaries sometimes cite disturbing first-century examples. Several are collated in Gupta, *1–2 Thessalonians*, 79–80; Jeffrey A. D. Weima, *1–2 Thessalonians*, BECNT 13 (Grand Rapids, MI: Baker Academic, 2014), 261–63.

> For this is the will of God
> = your sanctification [or holiness]
> = that you abstain from sexual immorality
> = that each one of you know how to control his own body . . .
> = that no one transgress and wrong his brother [or sister].

While there are many debated nuances, the piling up of related phrases spells out a clear equation. God is pleased by believers' holiness—conforming to the family likeness and upholding the family reputation—and one key family value is sexual self-control. We see this standard instilled throughout Scripture, as in the equally blunt command of 1 Corinthians 6:18: "Flee from sexual immorality."[8]

If pleasing God by conforming to his express will were insufficient, the apostles add three further motivations in 4:6–8. Jeffrey Weima insightfully observes the naming of each person of the Trinity and the three "tenses" of the Christian journey: believers should separate themselves from sexual immorality because of the past call of God, the present gift of the Holy Spirit, and the future judgment of the Lord Jesus.[9]

## To Walk and to Please God—in Social Conduct

In some church traditions, sexual propriety is the start and end—the sum total—of holy behavior. We are right to give it due attention because of its importance to God and to humans (1 Cor. 6:18–20), although perhaps Scripture gives it such a prominent place because it is such a countercultural call. Our apostolic church planters also draw attention to the impact of sanctification and holiness in additional domains of life. They raise some of these matters in letters to other churches, such as to those planted in nearby Philippi and Corinth.

---

8  One major commentary judges this sentiment prominent enough to structure the entire letter of 1 Corinthians around it, paired with the equally forceful "Flee from idolatry" (1 Cor. 10:14). Roy E. Ciampa and Brian S. Rosner, *The First Letter to the Corinthians*, PNTC (Grand Rapids, MI: Eerdmans, 2010).
9  Weima, *1–2 Thessalonians*, 252, 263, 277–83.

For God's church in Thessalonica, the next domain concerns social conduct inside and outside the church (1 Thess. 4:9–12).

It's tricky to get a handle on what the apostles are addressing here. Gupta's recent survey captures the primary options but reaches only (very) tentative conclusions.[10] Several relationships are in view: relationships within the Thessalonian church, relationships between believers in Thessalonica and those throughout the Macedonian region, and even relationships between church members and "outsiders." These multiple relational dimensions then complicate the generalized remarks about loving and living and working. We're not quite certain what *questions* are being addressed.

But the *answers* are sufficiently clear, even if we must be cautious about how to adapt them today. The grammar of the paragraph presents a topic sentence, a series of aspirations, and two reasons for pursuing them.

The general topic concerns "brotherly love" (4:9)—one of the Bible's five occurrences of the Greek word *philadelphia*. The Thessalonians are already performing well both among themselves and around the region. Nor is this a practice taught merely by the church-planting apostles but effectively by God himself, perhaps alluding to the commands of Jesus (Mark 12:28–34; John 13:34; 15:12, 17).

This positive reinforcement grounds the four ensuing instructions. Each instruction appears to narrow in scope, suggesting that our authors start with wider praise only to zero in on the specific problem they want to spotlight.[11] (1) Just as the Thessalonians already demonstrate brotherly love in various contexts, they should do so even more. (2) They should work hard at living quietly. This cautions not the noisy but the nosy, which corresponds with the instruction in the next letter (2 Thess. 3:11–12). (3) The same notion is brought out more directly in the third instruction: "Mind your own business" (1 Thess. 4:11 CSB, NIV). (4) Our authors reach their most specific application: the

10   Nijay K. Gupta, *1 & 2 Thessalonians*, ZCINT 13 (Grand Rapids, MI: Zondervan Academic, 2019), 130–39.

11   Weima, *1–2 Thessalonians*, 284.

Thessalonians should get to work, just as the apostles had previously instructed.

The call to action remains clear, even if the underlying causes of inaction are opaque. Nor is it clear how many within the church need this instruction. Again, this opacity invites prudent reflection before we thoughtlessly apply the apostolic responses, perhaps by demanding that everyone must have a paid income or that no believer dare seek support inside or outside the church. On the contrary, when the Thessalonians are commended for their brotherly love and then commanded to increase it, that love almost certainly includes generous giving to local and regional believers in need. The apostles are condemning not so much charity being given as charity being sought for inadequate reasons. Wider issues may also be in view, bringing the church into disrepute through raucous political involvement or offensive evangelism instead of quiet labor.

Our interpretation and application should be consistent with the two *reasons* for resuming work then given in 4:12. (1) Quiet labor maintains the key goal of appropriate conduct ("so that you may walk properly")—and not just before God but in everyone's eyes ("before outsiders"). (2) Providing for oneself means not being dependent on others, presumably either inside or outside the church.[12]

Apart from these instructions about appropriate conduct within the church community—and between church communities nearer and farther—we must not overlook the fleeting mention of walking properly "before outsiders." We return to this matter in more detail shortly. Already we might observe that the apostles do not envisage a church-led state, as occurred later at moments in Christendom, but rather God's humble people working quietly on the fringes. Such a sentiment will warm some and offend others, as the role of believers in society and politics has been debated throughout church history.

This is an appropriate place to pause our study of 1 Thessalonians 4–5 and note the one extended discussion of behavior in the second letter.

---

12  One example of careful weighing of interpretive options and application is Michael W. Holmes, *1 and 2 Thessalonians*, NIVAC (Grand Rapids, MI: Zondervan, 1998), 139–45.

Similar concerns about quiet work are elaborated on in 2 Thessalonians 3:6–15, and the repetition may suggest that some Thessalonians had trouble putting prior teaching into practice.

A key notion here concerns those who are "idle." Some English translations may give the impression that idleness is simply the absence of work: "For we hear that some among you walk in idleness, not busy at work, but busybodies" (3:11; cf. CSB, NRSV). But this is a more sinister term than a mere "loafer," seen in the following observations:

- In 3:6 and 3:11 we again see "walking" language (which also framed 1 Thess. 4:1–12). Our authors worry about a lifestyle habit, not an occasional rest day.
- There's the clever wordplay in English and Greek: "not busy at work, but busybodies" (2 Thess. 3:11). Those in view are not inactive but active—and doing something distasteful.
- The following verse (3:12) commands much the same resolution as 1 Thessalonians 4:11: "to do their work quietly and to earn their own living."
- This then suggests a link, or at least a parallel, with the motivations spelled out in 1 Thessalonians 4:12. Some church members are not yet walking properly before outsiders or are remaining inappropriately dependent on others (or both).

Interpreters thus agree that the apostles are targeting those who are actively "unruly" or "undisciplined" or "disorderly" (as the NASB translates verses such as 1 Thess. 5:14; 2 Thess. 3:6, 7, 11). To keep the contrast with working, the NIV describes such agitators as "idle and disruptive."

Two further features of 2 Thessalonians 3:6–15 are worth noting. First, the apostles not only invoke their prior teaching on the topic but also appeal to their prior modeling as self-supporting workers (3:7–9). There is more to say about modeling in our later chapter on leadership. Second, while the earlier letter encouraged the congregation *directly* about working quietly, here the apostles are addressing the congregation *about* a subset of them who are not yet laboring thus. The "unruly" minority are described in third-person language. The bulk of the congregation are (1) given instruction for dealing with the rebellious members of the church family; (2) implicitly praised, presumably for diligently complying with earlier teaching; and (3) encouraged to keep doing the right thing. The instruction of 3:13 matches other encouragements in Thessalonians to persist in godly behavior: "Do not grow weary in doing good." The same sentiment is found in another potentially early Pauline letter in almost the same words, where tireless doing of good within God's family also keeps one eye on aiding the wider community (Gal. 6:9–10).

## To Walk and to Please God—in Patient Expectation

Galatians joins the letters to the Thessalonians in calling for persistence: "Let us not grow weary of doing good" (Gal. 6:9). Again, we are encouraged to train believing brothers and sisters in long-term endurance, and we are challenged to avoid misselling the gospel message in an era of instant gratification. Galatians 6:7–10 compels good doing by promising that eventually, "in due season we will reap [eternal life], if we do not give up." David deSilva comments,

> The person who wants instant gratification for his or her labors cannot be a farmer. Similarly, the Christian journey calls for ongoing investment of oneself, one's resources, one's energies, promising its most significant rewards at a distant, future time. It calls for the manifestation of another variety of the Spirit's fruit, namely, patience.[13]

As we return to the instructions on lifestyle behavior in 1 Thessalonians 4–5, we find this same expectation of perseverance. And we see again the pastoral need for church leaders and church members alike to encourage other believers in the long-haul journey.

---

13  David A. deSilva, *The Letter to the Galatians*, NICNT (Grand Rapids, MI: Eerdmans, 2018), 495.

We have noted that all these instructions have stemmed from the climax of the first part of the letter. There the apostles report their prayers to visit the Thessalonians once again and "supply what is lacking in [their] faith" for their ongoing growth (3:10). They then pray directly for that reconnection (3:11) and that the Thessalonian believers might "increase and abound in love for one another and for all" and be established "blameless in holiness" before God at Jesus's return (3:12–13). We are hardly surprised that the letter then calls for a "walk" that pleases God, loving the Christian family through holiness in sexual and social conduct (4:1–12).

In what follows, the apostles change gears slightly, with deepening discussion of the future return of the Lord Jesus. They elaborate on the mechanics of Jesus's return for the dead (4:13–18), which we investigate in the next chapter. And then they resume the theme of how the living must wait in patient expectation (5:1–11).

The message is as easy to comprehend as it is arduous to live out. Images of two lifestyles are intertwined, complicated by a patchwork of metaphors. The interwoven illustrations all serve the same simple end: believers should be ready for Jesus's return in a way that unbelievers won't be.

The opening verses follow a familiar trajectory (5:1–3). The apostles assure the Thessalonians that they are already familiar with the gist, and indeed, much of the imagery is commonplace throughout the Bible and Paul's teachings. The foremost analogy here, which gives birth to further metaphors, is the surprise arrival of a thief in the night (cf. Matt. 24:42–44; 2 Pet. 3:10; Rev. 3:1–3; 16:15). Jesus's abrupt return will herald the day of the Lord and all it entails.

Unbelievers will be surprised and caught off guard. The pending verses paint them as complacent, living in darkness, asleep, drunk (1 Thess. 5:4–11). Most of the imagery reinforces the sense of being unprepared. A little of it hints at dissolute living (cf. Luke 21:34–36; 1 Pet. 4:1–5), and such undertones are further used to provoke Christians to a God-worthy lifestyle.

Believers will be surprised by the timing but will ideally be prepared. The apostles prepare believers *not* to be otherwise surprised, just as

Jesus instructed his followers to "stay awake" and "keep watch" in Matthew 24:36–25:13 and elsewhere. Images contrasting with the inattentive unbelievers tumble one over another as Christians are painted as children of light and of day—those who anticipate *the* pending day of the Lord. Accordingly, the Thessalonians should continue in "daylight" behavior: being awake and sober. This core command to vigilant sobriety in 1 Thessalonians 5:6 is repeated again in 5:8. Literal drunkenness is decried throughout Scripture, and the apostles have in view here a wider figurative range of sensible, self-controlled, holy living (cf. 1 Cor. 15:34; 2 Tim. 4:5; 1 Pet. 4:7–11). Godly behavior is appropriate in light of the famous Pauline triad. The Thessalonians already express their faith and love, and their hope remains focused on the salvation to be finalized at Jesus's return. Our authors once again celebrate this pending return and the completion of salvation, unpacking the majesty of God's plan and Jesus's death for believers both living and dead (1 Thess. 5:9–10). Just as the apostles themselves have been doing throughout this section and this letter, and just as they command in surrounding passages (4:18; 5:14), they again exhort the Thessalonians to be self-sustaining through mutual encouragement (5:11). Church members are to nurture one another, to "build up" each other (anticipating Paul's memorable language from 1 Corinthians and Acts 20:32). Once again the Thessalonians are both praised for and spurred on in their promising start: "just as you are doing."

The same enduring perseverance applies to the few instructions that pepper the second letter. Although they come expanded with discussions of present prayers and future judgments—topics we return to in later chapters—any injunctions in 2 Thessalonians effectively boil down to that same encouragement: "just as you are doing." Some of these encouragements are more indirect than direct. Consider the following highlights concerning behavior:

- The opening chapter is a prayer that thanks God for the Thessalonians. The authors report, "We . . . give thanks to God for you . . . because your faith is growing abundantly, and the love of every one of you for one another is increasing"; they add, "We ourselves boast about . . . your steadfastness and faith in all your persecutions and in the afflictions that you are enduring" (2 Thess. 1:3–4). The bulk of the chapter implies that the believers should persist in these virtues.

- We have already noted the prayers of 1:11–12 and 2:16–17, which ask that God would facilitate the Thessalonians' already God-worthy desires and deeds.
- Detailed teaching in the second chapter is fomented by the singular hope that the church not be "quickly shaken in mind or alarmed" or deceived about Jesus's return (2:1–3). Nestled among various thanksgivings and prayers for such steadfast persistence, some of the few direct instructions of the second letter appear: "Stand firm and hold to the traditions that you were taught by us" (2:15). No doubt, more activist believers may be frustrated at such calls to stay put and toe the party line, and we can certainly find these calls throughout the New Testament.[14]
- We have already considered the detailed concerns of 3:6–15, that the obedient majority respond helpfully to the rebellious nonworkers among them who have not yet complied with prior teaching.

We can easily concur that the second letter is basically another series of exhortations to stay the course. When the course is long, arduous, and countercultural, encouraging cheers from coaches and teammates are essential.

## Succinct Instructions

When we return to 1 Thessalonians, this habitual lifestyle ("walk") has already detailed matters of sexual and social conduct (4:1–12), an encouragement about the fate of the deceased (4:13–18), and a more general call to persistent godly living until Jesus's return (5:1–11). All

14  It is valuable to realize how persistently the New Testament repeats the call to stand firm; see, e.g., Acts 14:21–22; 1 Cor. 16:13; Phil. 1:27–28; 4:1; Col. 1:21–23; 2 Tim. 1:13–14; 3:14–15; Titus 1:7–9; 2 John 8–9; Rev. 2:4–5; 3:10–11; cf. Eph. 6:11–14; 1 Thess. 3:8; 1 Tim. 4:16; Heb. 10:32–36; 1 Pet. 5:8–9; Rev. 13:10; 14:12.

believers benefit from these instructions in Scripture, especially when they elaborate on conduct that pleases God. These are obviously also matters specifically relevant to the young church in Thessalonica, even though we cannot always reconstruct their exact circumstances.

The remainder of 1 Thessalonians 5 is a medley of short commands. As Abraham Malherbe notes, "The entire section [has] the appearance of a collection of unconnected gnomic sentences haphazardly strung together. The style should not, however, lead to the misperception that the sentences are not related to each other or to the situation in Thessalonica."[15] That is, we shouldn't think that these are random, timeless truths to be read and applied as a miscellany of proverbs. As with all Scripture, these commands' first-century specificity needs to be thoughtfully contextualized for various twenty-first-century settings. They differ from prior instructions only in their brevity, which of course can make it harder to comprehend and contextualize them. My goal here is to get a taste for what they contribute to the overall picture of persistent godly living without unpacking each in detail.

Commentators recognize that while some letters do conclude with fairly generic instructions, those here echo the more detailed directives already given. Scholars variously emphasize the prior calls for the Thessalonians to grow in faith/faithfulness (3:10), to live out their sanctification/holiness (e.g., 3:11–4:2; 4:3–8), to love one another (4:9–10), or to encourage and build up each other (4:18; 5:11). If my survey of the apostles' expectations of the Thessalonians is at all persuasive, we should appreciate that these options are in no way mutually exclusive. Pleasing God and nurturing his church in this pursuit are closely aligned, just as Jesus tightly links love of God and love of neighbor (Matt. 22:37–40; Luke 10:27–28).

We return in a later chapter to consider the role of local congregational leaders. Here the congregation is urged to respect and esteem them (1 Thess. 5:12–13). While a call to peace is often an independent injunction concerning whole congregations (e.g., Mark 9:50; Rom. 12:18; 2 Cor. 13:11; Heb. 12:14), its placement and wording here hint that this call concerns peace between congregants and leaders—or at least peace among congregants for their leaders' sake.

The terse instructions to the congregation in 1 Thessalonians 5:14 probably summarize the detailed directives in prior passages. While we cannot be absolutely certain, there are plausible grounds to read the next three instructions this way. "Admonish the idle" likely alludes to those who are failing to support themselves through work (4:9–12), using the terms that certainly address the unruly in 2 Thessalonians 3. "Encourage the fainthearted" accords reasonably with those uncertain about Jesus's return (1 Thess. 4:13–18). This hints that "Help the weak" refers to those struggling to persist expectantly in the meantime (5:1–11). The ensuing command to "be patient" is then yet another repeat of the recurrent charge to keep encouraging each other (4:18; 5:11). (This reading makes the ESV's "Be patient with *them* all" too restrictive; we might favor other translations' rendering that we are to be patient "with *everyone*" in the church.) That sense of mutual edification is extended in 5:15, again with one eye also on the wider community beyond the church.

General edifying behavior continues in the next bursts of instructions. These are two single sentences in Greek, most clearly captured by the NASB, and they say more about communal worship than private piety. "The will of God in Christ Jesus" includes persistent rejoicing, praying, and thanksgiving (5:16–18). And Spirit-fueled prophecies should be permitted and appraised (5:19–22). Because both sentences concern the congregation's interactions with God, we return to them in chapter 5.

Even the closing lines of the first letter include brief commands in keeping with the letter's concerns (5:23–28).[16] The believers are to pray for the authors. They are to greet each other with a "holy" kiss: one

---

16  See especially the detailed analysis of Weima, whose specialty is letters' conclusions. *1–2 Thessalonians*, 413–32.

suited to the people of God privileged with past, present, and future sanctification. The kindred term "brothers and sisters" (ESV mg.) is overtly included each time and echoes the call to peaceful family living found in parts of the letter (e.g., 5:13). The sanctified greeting is to extend to "all" the brothers and sisters. This also explains the third injunction, that "all" in the church family hear this letter. These three commands are wrapped in prayers that underscore the letter's themes. God, the source of peace, is invoked to continue his sanctifying work in the Thessalonians as they persist until Jesus's return, as the grace of the Lord Jesus Christ is also invoked.

### Concerns for Others

These observations from the closing of the first letter reinforce how the apostles are concerned with communal life within God's church. Christians are to journey together and nurture each other along the way (e.g., Rom. 15:1–7; Gal. 6:1–2; Heb. 3:12–14; 12:12–13; James 5:19–20; Jude 20–23). The Thessalonian letters, as much as any other part of the Bible, expose the inadequacy of the increasingly popular maxim that we play *only* for "an audience of one."

#### Concern for the Local Congregation

Many of our observations have understandably noted the concern the Thessalonians should show each other. A quick recap reminds us that they are to keep abounding in love for one another (1 Thess. 3:12; 4:9–10; 2 Thess. 1:3), encouraging and edifying each other (1 Thess. 4:18; 5:11), caring for those in various situations of need and doing good (1 Thess. 5:14–15; 2 Thess. 3:13–15), and not causing harm (1 Thess. 4:6).

#### Concern for the Wider Church

I am distressed to visit churches that, for all practical purposes, behave as if their local congregation is basically coterminous with the people of God. Prayers are made only for local believers; members away from home don't think to visit another gathering. Other New

Testament letters show overt awareness of believers in other parts of God's world, seen in the sharing of greetings (e.g., Rom. 16:16; 1 Cor. 16:19–20; Phil. 4:21–22; Heb. 13:24; 1 Pet. 5:13; 2 John 13; 3 John 14) and the sharing of financial resources (e.g., Rom. 15:25–27; 1 Cor. 16:1–4). The same camaraderie is glimpsed in Thessalonians, although as one of Paul's midcareer church plants, the Thessalonian church is unsurprisingly part of a less established network.

The first key example is 1 Thessalonians 1:6–10. In three sentences the missionaries joyfully recount the Thessalonians' original conversion, with each sentence recalling something of their transformation and its impact on the wider church. (1) The Thessalonians "became imitators of us and of the Lord," with the result that they "became an example to all the believers in Macedonia and in Achaia"—that is, both northern and southern Greece (1:6–7). They exemplify joyful persistence in the face of affliction (cf. 2:14–15; 3:1–5). (2) In turn, "the word of the Lord sounded forth from you in Macedonia and Achaia," and "your faith in God has gone forth everywhere" (1:8). The result is that the missionaries don't need to report the Thessalonians' dramatic conversion: that news has traveled fast! (3) Consequently, other believers are familiar with the Thessalonians' transformation, and they "keep talking about" it (1:9 NLT). This impact on the wider church is almost certainly unintentional, and perhaps such passive elements require us to think all the more intentionally about how news of our initial conversion and subsequent behavior would be perceived by believers elsewhere. I sometimes pray that Western churches will not only work hard at sending cross-cultural workers to outside nations but will also fare well at listening to cross-cultural voices from outside their own echo chambers.

A more active concern for other believers is on show in a second example. The mention in 4:9–10 is fleeting but significant. The authors are confident in the Thessalonians' "brotherly love" because such love is on display within the congregation *and* "toward all the brothers and sisters in the entire region of Macedonia" (CSB). We might speculate that the Thessalonians are offering hospitality to believers who visit or relocate to this thriving regional capital. Certainly, we read many other examples of hospitality expected of believers (e.g., Rom. 12:13; 15:22–29; 16:1–2; Philem. 22; Heb. 13:1–2; 1 Pet. 4:9; 3 John 5–8). Perhaps having seen the Philippian believers supporting the Pauline mission in Thessalonica (Phil. 4:14–16), the Thessalonians themselves are now contributing to the subsequent mission in Corinth (2 Cor. 11:7–9). Over the next half decade, believers in the region regularly contribute to Paul's collection for the churches in Judea (Rom. 15:26; 2 Cor. 8:1–5); perhaps Paul is already collecting, or perhaps generous Thessalonians are already at work alleviating the "extreme poverty" among believers throughout Macedonia (2 Cor. 8:2). Commentators find it telling that the praise of widespread love in 1 Thessalonians 4:9–10 is immediately followed by the narrowing commands to buckle down and earn a living (cf. Eph. 4:28).

Just as we hear the apostles later boasting about Macedonian generosity, they also report boasting to other churches of the Thessalonians' steadfastness and faith during persistent persecution and afflictions (2 Thess. 1:4). The local church makes a wider impact.

## Concern for Wider Society

As today's post-Christendom West continues to segregate church and state, religion is increasingly portrayed as a private matter. We must remember that the now-familiar term "church" (Gk. *ekklēsia*) simply meant "an assembly," in the same way that we speak today of a sporting or social "club": people gathering around a shared interest. Certainly, the countercultural behaviors of this first-century association couldn't go unnoticed—just as Israel, God's Old Testament *ekklēsia*, was "singled out" as God's special treasure for public display (e.g., Ex. 19:5–6; Lev. 20:22–26; 1 Kings 8:52–53 NASB).[17]

---

17  Christopher J. H. Wright, *The Mission of God's People: A Biblical Theology of the Church's Mission*, BTFL (Grand Rapids, MI: Zondervan, 2010), 123–26, 129–32; Andy Johnson, *1 and 2 Thessalonians*, THNTC (Grand Rapids, MI: Eerdmans, 2016), 32–33, 112–16, 234–36. Alert commentators note many places where the Thessalonian letters apply Old Testament allusions to the Thessalonian believers.

Throughout this chapter, I have been careful to draw attention to various indications that believers are to keep one eye on the reputation of God's church with outsiders. One goal of quiet labor is to "walk properly before outsiders" (1 Thess. 4:11–12; cf. perhaps 2 Thess. 3:13). Retribution is to be forsaken in favor of "always pursu[ing] what is good for one another and for all" (1 Thess. 5:15 CSB). We can now add the apostles' prayer that the Thessalonians "increase and abound in love for one another and for all" (3:12).

The New Testament makes several such mentions of Christians' reputation with outsiders, although these are typically brief and easily missed. The equally brief Thessalonian comments contribute to a theology of everyday conduct within eyeshot of society. Of course, some instructions about "winning behavior" are concerned with winning outsiders to the gospel message (e.g., 1 Cor. 9:19–23; 1 Pet. 3:1–6). But churches are often reminded of good conduct without such motives (Gal. 6:9–10; Col. 4:5–6). The instructions are most often anxious that God's people not cause offense but garner a positive reputation (Matt. 5:14–16; 1 Cor. 10:32–33; 1 Tim. 3:7; Titus 2:1–10; 1 Pet. 2:12). This often includes living up to societal expectations where possible (Rom. 12:17–18; cf. 2 Cor. 8:20–21) and keeping a low profile (Titus 3:1–2). Many of these latter ideals are in view in 1 Thessalonians 4:9–12.

And although it might be overreach, a majority of interpreters think the language of 1 Thessalonians 1:8 alludes to some kind of public evangelism. Those people "everywhere" reporting about the Thessalonians' transformation are not existing believers but unbelievers! James Ware argues that "the Thessalonians had not only received the apostle's message, but were also themselves active in communicating it to others."[18]

## Concern for God

Undeniably, God's opinions also matter. Verses like 1 Thessalonians 2:4 acknowledge the principle that the apostles speak "not to please people,

---

18  James Ware, "The Thessalonians as a Missionary Congregation: 1 Thessalonians 1,5–8," *ZNW* 83 (1992): 127; cf. Gary S. Shogren, *1 & 2 Thessalonians*, ZECNT 13 (Grand Rapids, MI: Zondervan, 2012), 70–71.

but rather God" (CSB). My intent has been to show that Thessalonians joins many other parts of Scripture in teaching that we don't perform *only* for an audience of one. Some Christian temperaments habitually underscore passages that pit God against society (e.g., Acts 5:29; Gal. 1:10; Eph. 6:5–6). This can lead all too easily to an "us versus them" mentality, in which we quickly ignore or demonize "them"—all under the guise of pious concern for God. On the whole, the Thessalonian letters deny that the choice is mutually exclusive. They affirm the priority of walking to please God—and they show that this aim typically *includes* walking to please and care for others, even those beyond the church.

Christians journey toward an end goal. God's declaration of holiness marks the beginning of that journey, and that same declaration provides confidence for his final judgment (e.g., 1 Thess. 3:13; 5:23). Our next chapter explores what we can expect at that time. As we await Jesus's return, our sanctified status heralds the family likeness and the family reputation and expects us to walk accordingly.

3

# Until the Coming of the Lord

## The End of (Current) Earthly Life

THESSALONIANS IS PROBABLY best known for its *eschatology*—what it teaches about "the last things." Some readers may know these letters only because of a famous funeral passage, a potential contribution to popular rapture theology, or speculation about other "end times" elements. Thessalonians is certainly concerned about what happens at the end of a Christian's current earthly journey.

Already some of the jargon of the foregoing paragraph makes some presuppositions that deserve checking. Among them, we might clarify (1) what we understand by "end times" language, (2) how detailed or systematic a picture the Thessalonian letters paint for us, and even (3) whether Christians depart the earth at Jesus's second coming.

We reflect on such issues throughout this chapter. It is important to acknowledge that our apostolic collaborators' focus on "last things" is not an end in itself. Their repeated mention of eschatological matters is designed to influence how the Thessalonians live *now*. When hectic Westerners were discovering the need for life coaches, Stephen Covey wrote an insanely best-selling crossover from business management to life management: *The 7 Habits of Highly Effective People.*[1] These habits

---

1 Stephen R. Covey, *The 7 Habits of Highly Effective People* (New York: Free Press, 1989).

codified commonsense practices, with the second habit articulating, "Begin with the end in mind." That is, live today in such a way that correlates with and contributes to your expectations of tomorrow. The eschatology of Thessalonians is similarly focused on making a difference now rather than fueling speculation about the future. Some future certainties are confirmed: Jesus returns to earth and finalizes God's judgments. These are further motivations for the holy living and persistence that we surveyed in our prior chapter.

## A Repeated Reminder

I have already hinted at a couple of famous passages, and we turn to those shortly. Especially if we're familiar with only those passages, it is valuable to pause and realize just how drenched the letters are with such forward-looking sentiments. Our authors invoke Jesus's return and God's judgment multiple times to explain God's past actions (our initial sanctification/conversion) and to motivate believers' present living (persistent growth in holy conduct).

If we reprise figure 1 from the introduction, we can shade all the places where eschatology is invoked. The result is seen in figure 2 and highlights that along with some concentrated major sections, mention of Jesus's return often falls at the end of a chapter—especially each chapter of 1 Thessalonians.

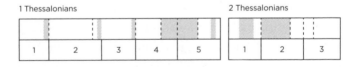

Figure 2   Eschatological passages in Thessalonians

Such a figure alerts us to matters of language. Our letters are almost entirely bereft of "last things" language. There's but one mention of "at last" (1 Thess. 2:16), which probably looks forward to God's future judgment of those who oppose the Christian gospel. There is no whiff of the actual terminology from which we derive English expressions like "last days" or "eschatology" (e.g., Gk. *eschatos*). Most relevant passages, however, including those that climax each chapter, do use the Greek word *parousia*, usually translated "coming," which has worked its way into the language of some church traditions. While I occasionally slip into popular terminology, our letters' contributors are clearly more interested in Jesus's "arrival" than in any other language of "the end."

This prominent focus on how the triune God will return and wrap up current earthly history is lost on neither scholars nor pastors. One of the most technical commentaries calculates that "over a quarter of 1 Thessalonians and nearly half of 2 Thessalonians deal with problems and issues regarding the parousia or coming of Christ from heaven."[2] And in a series of popular introductions to Bible books, Warren Wiersbe attempts to distill the message of each to a single two-word command. The book of Leviticus is summarized as *Be Holy*; Job is said to teach *Be Patient*; Philippians aids us to *Be Joyful*. It is no surprise that the Thessalonian letters are compressed to the simple message *Be Ready*.[3]

Our visual representation of the letters' eschatology also identifies the two concentrated sections of teaching, one in each letter. We turn to each major passage before synthesizing the contributions of the two letters in their entirety.

## 1 Thessalonians 4:13-18

We don't actually know why the first letter suddenly interrupts discussion of holy living (1 Thess. 4:1-12) with mention of Jesus's future arrival. The best speculation is that upon his recent return from Thessalonica (3:6), Timothy has brought some question from the Thessalonians or reported his own observation of their confusion. Commentators disagree as to whether many believers have died or just a few, whether they died from natural causes or martyrdom, and even precisely why the survivors are distraught. But all interpreters concur

---

2   Charles A. Wanamaker, *The Epistles to the Thessalonians*, NIGTC (Grand Rapids, MI: Eerdmans, 1990), 10.

3   Warren W. Wiersbe, *Be Ready: Living in Light of Christ's Return; 1 & 2 Thessalonians* (Colorado Springs: David C. Cook, 2010).

that the Thessalonians are somehow distressed at what this means for the deceased saints' standing before God in the future.[4]

Akin to virtually every passage in every New Testament letter, the apostolic response cherry-picks some relevant highlights to pastorally address the congregation's immediate needs. It's not that Paul and Silvanus and Timothy interrupt their broadcast for a systematic class on doctrine. They are not mapping out every step of Jesus's return in precision order and exhaustive detail. (When Paul and Sosthenes write a few years later to the church at Corinth, they select details that are similar but not identical, such as those in 1 Cor. 15:51–52.)

This pastoral angle leads the passage. Although our authors use a common rhetorical introduction, it's employed to relieve the Thessalonian believers from "griev[ing] as others do who have no hope" (1 Thess. 4:13). The passage concerns "those who sleep in death"; this phrasing from the NIV neatly captures both the idiom and its meaning. Indeed, while "sleeping" is a common euphemism in the ancient world, it's a fortuitous one for Christians: dead believers' bodies will one day be awakened. In our prior chapter, we saw several examples in which Christian lifestyle is contrasted with non-Christian conduct. The apostles' current discussion of the pending arrival of Jesus moves shortly to make such contrasts (5:4–8). Already here (4:13–18) Christian grief for dead believers should not express hopelessness as non-Christian grief might.

The basis for hope is the status that deceased believers will experience at Jesus's parousia. Again, we should recognize that the passage isn't especially focused on Jesus's itinerary or the fate of Christians still alive at that time. Deceased believers are not permanently, as we might say today, "dead and buried" or "done and dusted." They are not forgotten in God's economy. Several points of the passage are cross-culturally foreign to Western readers, and unpacking these reminds us that the apostles are addressing first-century Mediterranean concerns—and

---

4    Nijay Gupta sharply spots that the pastoral response is not assurance about the *current* standing or circumstances of the deceased. *1–2 Thessalonians*, NCCS (Eugene, OR: Cascade, 2016), 93.

that they are providing responses to issues that almost certainly differ in their specifics from our own concerns.[5] As objectively as any of us can, commentators reconstruct the key highlights of 1 Thessalonians 4:13–18 as follows.

In most cultures in most eras, an expected visiting dignitary isn't left ungreeted. He doesn't reach the portcullis of a castle or the gates of a city or the foyer of a chamber of government, only to knock, twiddle his thumbs, and wait for someone to open up and belatedly acknowledge his arrival. Even today we are familiar with the way that host-leaders go out to the port of entry to meet and escort the visitor. Local citizens are also swept up in the welcome, perhaps lining major boulevards to cheer the passing motorcade. Visitor and welcomers alike might describe being "honored" to participate. Distinguished citizens might be further honored by being invited to a special "reception" with the visiting dignitary.

This kind of language seems to be exactly what is used in our passage. "The coming of the Lord [Jesus]" will be noisily heralded: "with a cry of command, with the voice of an archangel, and with the sound of the trumpet of God" (4:15–16). Dead believers will be raised to join those still alive. All believers, "together," will head out "to meet the Lord" (4:17). (Mention of "clouds" and "air" are not unimportant, but they're background set dressing.) It is true that this gathering is left hanging midair, as it were. Some modern traditions assume that Jesus then whisks his faithful flock back to heaven. But the ancient language commonly implies that the visiting dignitary and welcomers alike return back to the *welcomers'* territory. For example, Josephus recounts a Jewish high priest fearing the arrival of Alexander the Great. God assures the priest in a dream, charging him to festoon Jerusalem, open its gates, marshal the priests in dress uniform, and head out to effect the meeting. The priest joyfully complies and awaits "the coming of the

---

5    The introduction to an accessible study of end-times speculation surveys how the eschatological fervor of any era tends to be self-interested, skewing the way we read eschatological passages. Matthew L. Halsted, *The End of the World as You Know It: What the Bible Really Says about the End Times (and Why It's Good News)* (Bellingham, WA: Lexham, 2023).

king," ushering him back into the city. Josephus uses a near-identical word for "meeting" (Gk. *hypantēsis*) as Thessalonians (Gk. *apantēsis*) and also uses the common term for the "coming/arrival" of the king (Gk. *parousia*).[6] If a biblical parallel carries more weight than Josephus, as Paul draws close to Rome at the end of Acts, we see Roman believers travel dozens of miles out to meet him and escort him back (Acts 28:15, again using Gk. *apantēsis*).

The major evangelical commentators I've interacted with are all but unanimous in this interpretation. And again, the apostles are not emphasizing Jesus's precise GPS coordinates at every step but assuring the Thessalonians that their deceased friends and family will be fully honored participants in the welcoming cavalcade. Twice the Thessalonians are assured that Jesus's arrival will be in company with resurrected believers (1 Thess. 4:14, 16). Twice the Thessalonians are assured of this fact's certainty: it accords with the doctrinal precedent of Jesus himself having died and risen (4:14), and the ensuing teaching is "a word from the Lord" (4:15)—probably a loose paraphrase of Jesus's teaching in Matthew 24:29–41 about his future return. Several times the apostles hint that the dead might even earn the *better* standing in this entourage. And the final clauses emphasize that all believers, both the (formerly) dead and the (already) living, will remain forever in the pleasure of the Lord's company. The Thessalonians should not grieve hopelessly but should encourage one another (1 Thess. 4:17–18)!

Sharp observers might note that figure 2 also shades 1 Thessalonians 5:1–11 as eschatologically focused. That chapter is certainly grounded in the unknown timing of Jesus's return. It draws attention to "the times and the seasons" and the fact that we cannot precisely define the timetable of the day of the Lord, which will come "like a thief in the night" (5:1–3). But even if this teaching about Jesus's return arrives abruptly (4:13), our authors steer the remainder of their discussion back to how believers should behave now in anticipation. For this reason,

---

6   Josephus, *Antiquities* 11.8.4–5, esp. §§325–28; also 13.4.4, §101; cf. Ben Witherington III, *1 and 2 Thessalonians: A Socio-Rhetorical Commentary* (Grand Rapids, MI: Eerdmans, 2006), 142–43.

I have already treated 5:1–11 in our prior chapter on present-day living. We're reminded that the apparently doctrinal section in 4:13–18 about Jesus's return is similarly crafted to influence the Thessalonians' *current* approach to life and death.

So we model responsible use of Scripture when we use this famous passage at Christian funerals, especially to assure mourners that Christian grief is shaped by hope. We are to use these words to encourage those who still live about how to live.

## 2 Thessalonians 2

The other extended discussion of Jesus's return is likewise concerned with how to live in the present. It fills most, if not all, of 2 Thessalonians 2. The parousia also grounds much of the preceding chapter, so we start there.

### 2 Thessalonians 1:3–12

The apostles open the second letter by thanking God for the Thessalonians' abounding faith and love. (Once more we see that "faith" has room to "grow phenomenally," as *The Message* captures the superlative, and that its effects should be visible.) We might expect "hope" to be named next, and it's surely at work. But the apostles continue to encourage this congregation by further praising their steadfast perseverance and (again) faith in the midst of persecutions and afflictions.

Most of this opening chapter is one long Greek sentence (2 Thess. 1:3–10). The bulk of it turns to assuring the Thessalonians that their suffering is a positive sign of God's kingdom plans rather than some negative reprimand. There is an undertone of vindication, assuring the congregation that their persecutors will be repaid with affliction and "will suffer the punishment of eternal destruction, away from the presence of the Lord and from the glory of his might" (1:9). Even more prominent is the assurance that the afflicted Thessalonians (and their apostles) will be granted relief and counted on God's side. Yet again readers are reminded that people can respond favorably or unfavorably to God and his gospel message, which is seen in their ensuing lifestyle (cf. 1 Thess. 2:13–16; 4:3–6; 5:4–8). The rest of the New Testament fleshes out this contrast with a gallery of images, from wheat versus weeds (Matt. 13:24–30) and sheep versus goats (Matt. 25:31–46) to the branded lackeys of the beast versus the designated courtiers of the Lamb (Rev. 13:11–14:5).

As throughout the New Testament, Thessalonians confirms that this binary sorting is dramatically finalized at the day of the Lord, a notion consistent also with Old Testament expectations. God's final, righteous judgment runs throughout 2 Thessalonians 1, and the chapter concludes with another prayer that God would continue to count the believers worthy of his calling and to cultivate the outward expressions of their faith—and thus that they would be honored ("glorified") in him (1:11–12; cf. 1 Thess. 2:12).

## 2 Thessalonians 2:1–12

The subsequent chapter keeps the same judgment day in view but moves to the question of its timing. Again, more than a pre-prepared doctrinal lecture, Paul and Silvanus and Timothy are pastorally responding to anxiety among their congregation. They may not spell out everything to our intellectual satisfaction, but we can glean some partial insights from this unique chapter.

The topic at hand is indeed "the coming of our Lord Jesus Christ and our being gathered together to him" (2 Thess. 2:1), and these events are viewed jointly and not as two separate occasions. The congregation is anxious because of a rumor circulating that "the day of the Lord has come" (2:2). We do not know why its arrival should unsettle the Thessalonians, but one good guess is that the rumor they've heard also suggests that the Thessalonians are slated for God's negative condemnation. The Old Testament speaks frequently of "the day of the LORD," when God will judge—often with his own people in the crosshairs (e.g., Joel 1:15–2:11; Amos 5:18–20; Zeph. 1:14–18). Jesus likewise warns that "on that day" many who address him as Lord will be pronounced "workers of lawlessness" and be excluded from the kingdom (Matt. 7:21–23; cf. Luke 13:22–30). The letter to the Hebrews certainly threatens that those who look like God's people may be judged his enemies (esp. Heb. 10:26–31; cf. Rev. 2:4–5, 20–23). Such a fear would explain why so much of 2 Thessalonians 1–2 repeats the apostles' confidence that this congregation is exhibiting positive fruit of salvation. Another fair guess is that the Thessalonians think some train of final events has been set in motion and that current earthly history will be wrapped up imminently. We have seen that Jesus's return *is* always potentially imminent (1 Thess. 5:1–3), but elsewhere Jesus warns not to confuse early signs and final denouement (e.g., Mark 13:3–8).

The apostles respond with several soothing strategies. Each of these is valuable, although one is most pertinent to our study here of eschatology. It takes up the balance of the chapter and provides evidence for the immediate, blunt command: "Let no one deceive you in any way" (2 Thess. 2:3). The apostolic response boils down to this command and a familiar script: events leading up to and through the day of the Lord are clear enough that they will not pass unnoticed (cf. Matt. 24:26–31; Rev. 1:7). Because certain events are yet to transpire, the Thessalonians need not fret that the day of the Lord has already arrived.

Interpreters observe a range of difficulties as we seek to squeeze further clarity from 2 Thessalonians 2:3–12, especially the fact that the apostles are summarizing teaching that Paul has already given the Thessalonians in person (2:5). We must read and teach cautiously here because we are "walking into the middle of a conversation between Paul and the Thessalonian believers, a dialogue with a rather extensive history."[7] Gary Shogren's additional imagery is instructive: "The modern reader must interpret the passage with only an incomplete knowledge of Paul's earlier teaching. We are confronted with a puzzle with pieces missing, but we are not sure how many there are or what they contain."[8] Interpreting any Bible passage involves our existing assumptions. Our current passage has no direct parallel, and end-times

7  Jeffrey A. D. Weima, *1–2 Thessalonians*, BECNT 13 (Grand Rapids, MI: Baker Academic, 2014), 507.
8  Gary S. Shogren, *1 & 2 Thessalonians*, ZECNT 13 (Grand Rapids, MI: Zondervan, 2012), 266.

teaching is especially emotive and pastoral and universally relevant. And we might come to it with a relatively blank slate or with a fervent theological system we expect Thessalonians to fit into. People from both vantage points need to be thoughtful about the additional puzzle pieces they assume and attempt to link. Conforming Thessalonians to a preconceived system is particularly fraught; we must be wary of trying to force pieces into an existing picture in which they may not quite align. And we are in the realm of apocalyptic language, where believers heavily disagree on the balance between "literal" and symbolic interpretation. There is little in our passage that clarifies this balance.[9]

What events do the apostles think must precede Jesus's parousia? Given the lack of detail within the passage and the lack of certain parallels to other passages, we are largely limited to echoing the highlights of the text itself. Later in this chapter, we consider potential links with wider biblical eschatology.

After their primary command ("Let no one deceive you in any way"), the apostles list the two noticeable precursors: "For that day will not come, unless the rebellion comes first, and the man of lawlessness is revealed" (2 Thess. 2:3). The intimation is that the Thessalonian readers and their Christian successors should be able to identify these events—though this does not necessarily mean that they will recognize these events the instant they begin (see below).

There is no further elaboration on "the rebellion." This English translation acknowledges that the Greek concept can apply to a range of political revolutions and military insurrections, and it's probably more comprehensible than jargonized "apostasy" (CSB, NASB). But most interpreters accept that in this context it likely warns of such a narrower sense of religious backsliding (e.g., 1 Tim. 4:1; Heb. 3:12; 2 Pet. 2:1–2).

We are told a little more about "the man of lawlessness." He's immediately given a second description, "the son of destruction" (2 Thess.

---

9   Even the simplest eschatological language isn't straightforward. What does it mean for Jesus to descend, and for every eye to see him, when the earth is spherical? Andy Johnson, *1 and 2 Thessalonians*, THNTC (Grand Rapids, MI: Eerdmans, 2016), 256.

2:3), a phrase that does not so much anticipate his own violent acts as his own violent end (2:8—see NIV, NRSV; cf. the same label for hapless Judas in John 17:12). Interpreters consistently see this individual as an antichrist figure.

This lawless one seeks to be the sole object of worship, usurping the roles of "every so-called god or object of worship" and even of the living and true God (2 Thess. 2:4). Interpreting the clause "He takes his seat in the temple of God" depends substantially on our view of apocalyptic language and apocalyptic events. Commentators basically reject the notion of a specific building (especially some future rebuilt temple in Jerusalem); the man of lawlessness sets himself up wherever humans exalt deities. This may well include setting himself up among the members of God's church, God's metaphorical temple.

The apostles don't give many other distinguishing features for picking this man of lawlessness out of a police lineup. The language echoes a range of Tyrian, Seleucid, and Roman rulers who had aspired to displace God (sometimes even in the Jerusalem temple). The generic description is enough to mollify the anxious Thessalonians but is insufficient for us to foresee which of many contenders may prove in time to be the climactic "incarnation" of this recurring type. (It's a bit like trying to gauge whether we've seen the final actor to reboot our favorite superhero.)

The language of "incarnation" is mine. There are certainly other terms in our passage that describe the figure in language comparable to Jesus. The man of lawlessness likewise has a "coming" and will be "revealed" (2:3, 6, 8, 9; for Jesus, see 1:7; 2:1, 8). We noted in chapter 1 that Satan energizes the man of lawlessness to work false signs and wonders to deceive those refusing to love the truth. This is potentially cast as the dark equivalent of God's empowerment of Jesus, although Thessalonians doesn't furnish such sentiment (see John 14.9–11; Acts 2:22; Heb. 2:4).

The parallels end there. A cardinal feature of the Bible's apocalyptic theology is that—unlike the drawn-out tension and last-minute resolution of contemporary movies—the forces of dark and light are *not* evenly matched. Some unspecified time after the man of lawlessness's parousia, Jesus's own parousia will defeat him instantly and effortlessly (2 Thess. 2:8).

In the meantime, and with equally frustrating brevity, we are told that the mystery of lawlessness is already making headway in the world, even while the man of lawlessness himself is currently restrained (2:6–7). Biblical "mystery" can include an "advance taste," recognized at least by God's people. But current restraint will be removed and the full main course of lawlessness will arrive (2:8). Unbelievers will remain deceived, which aligns people's choices, Satan's machinations, and God's ratification of their fate (2:9–12).[10]

Of course we crave more detail on all these elements! The assumed knowledge and tangled chronology of these verses don't help, much like a movie trailer offering only tantalizing snippets of the more detailed story to come. But the key points are transparent and warrant repeating. The apostles seek to calm Thessalonian consternation that the end (or some key harbinger) has already arrived. Their confidence is that the outworking of lawlessness is still in its early stages. There seems to be a final showdown that has not yet arrived.

Our apostles cleverly weave in some additional pastoral care. They acknowledge the forces of darkness: the influence of Satan and his protégé. This helps the Thessalonians accommodate the oppression that church planters and congregation alike have experienced (1 Thess. 1:6–7; 2:14–16, 18; 3:3–5; 2 Thess. 1:3–10; 3:1–3). And they are assured that God ultimately controls the forces of darkness and will easily snuff them out at a time of his choosing; such assurances constitute much of this latter letter (2 Thess. 1:5–10; 2:6–12; 3:1–5). Of course, these points

---

10  Alert or informed readers recognize a subtle difference between "*what* is restraining him now" and "*he* who now restrains." Commentators rightly ponder the myriad possibilities, generally concur that these are two facets of the *same* restraint, but admit that "Paul provides no further description of these entities, and little if any precedent for this language appears in prior sources." Timothy A. Brookins, *First and Second Thessalonians*, Paideia (Grand Rapids, MI: Baker Academic, 2021), 169. While our passage is uninterested in clarifying the restraint (or restraints), the last two decades have seen a marked move toward championing the archangel Michael; in detail, see Weima, *1–2 Thessalonians*, 567–77.

are repeated more broadly throughout the Bible, especially the assurance running through much of Revelation (e.g., Rev. 19:11–21; 21:1–8).

## 2 Thessalonians 2:13–17

Some interpreters and most Bible translations give the impression that 2 Thessalonians 2:13–17 begins a new phase in the letter. Even my heading here may reinforce that impression. Certainly, we find a change of tone after the darker focus of the preceding verses. But a good number of trustworthy commentators demonstrate how this passage rounds out the apostles' assurance.[11]

As at the start of the letter, the apostles again thank God for the certitude of the Thessalonians' standing in God's eyes (2:13–14). Such a prayer report is hardly necessary, especially when it all but duplicates that earlier thanksgiving. This repetition, its placement, and its content are informative. The assurances of the two opening chapters are not completely disjointed but are related: God will both vindicate his people and finally judge evil. So the apostles again rejoice in their confidence of which verdict their flock will receive: the Thessalonians are beloved by the Lord, chosen and called by God for salvation, destined for glory.

Then there's a direct, two-part command to "stand firm" and to "keep a strong grip on" the traditions taught by the apostles (2:15 NLT).

(This same structuring occurs in the corresponding section of the first letter. Two consecutive reflections on the return of Jesus [1 Thess. 4:13–18; 5:1–11] conclude with the same optimistic outlook for believers: "God has not destined us for wrath, but to obtain salvation through our Lord Jesus Christ" [5:9]. And the authors expect the Thessalonians to persist in such truths and to live in light of them [5:11 and beyond].)

This section closes with yet another example of section-ending prayers (2 Thess. 2:16–17). The apostles' recollection of God's love, comfort, and hope and their prayer for further comfort and strength in

---

11  For example, and in increasing detail, Johnson, *1 and 2 Thessalonians*, 181; Gordon D. Fee, *The First and Second Letters to the Thessalonians*, NICNT (Grand Rapids, MI: Eerdmans, 2009), 270, 297; Weima, *1–2 Thessalonians*, 489–90, 491–95.

perseverance work well in any setting. But the recollection and prayer make even more sense in the context of encouraging the Thessalonians that (1) they are already being shaped by God's work in saving them and (2) they should persist in the journey until Jesus's return.[12]

### Summary

We can thus see that the whole of 2 Thessalonians 2, if not chapters 1–2 together, present a coherent and helpful message—even if we cannot decode every detail. The content won't scratch our every eschatological itch, though we return in a moment to consider what can be affirmed. More than secret eschatological insights, the content's pastoral objective is what we should note. In addition to assuring those who persevere through opposition, the apostles take space to acknowledge and somewhat explain this opposition, including hostility experienced from other human beings. We recall that many biblical passages give space to such opposition to Christian believers, whether extended sections or recurrent motifs or myriad offhand reminders.[13] In short, we should affirm Jeffrey Weima's aphorism: "The apostle's overall goal or larger purpose remains quite clear: not to *predict* the future . . . but to *pastor* the Thessalonian church."[14]

---

12  I am not elsewhere unpacking 2 Thess. 3:1–5 in any detail. Commentators usually emphasize the change of style that transitions readers toward 3:6–15. Yet we might observe how 3:1–5 also recapitulates assurances and prayers for believers as they persist under opposition. Some commentators (e.g., Malherbe, Brookins) even structure 2:13–3:5 together.

13  *Extended sections:* Swaths of Mark's Gospel compile adjacent stories of mixed reactions to Jesus (e.g., Mark 2:1–4:34; 11:27–12:44). See also John 15:18–25 and similar. *Recurrent motifs:* The book of Acts is presented as (and arguably structured around) various internal and external threats to the expansion of the gospel message (e.g., Acts 3:1–4:31; 4:32–5:11; 8:1–9:31; 12:1–24; 15:1–16:5; 21:17–28:31). The book of Revelation persistently contrasts the fate of believers with the fate of "those who dwell on the earth" (Rev. 3:10; 6:10; 8:13; 11:10; 13:8, 12, 14; 17:2, 8). *Myriad reminders:* Memorable sound bites abound, such as "Many . . . walk as enemies of the cross of Christ" (Phil. 3:18); "All who desire to live a godly life in Christ Jesus will be persecuted" (2 Tim. 3:12); "Do not be surprised at the fiery trial when it comes upon you to test you, as though something strange were happening to you" (1 Pet. 4:12). See also Acts 14:22; Rom. 5:3–5; 1 Thess. 3:3; Heb. 12:5–11; James 1:2–4; 1 John 3:13. And these are merely New Testament samples.

14  Weima, *1–2 Thessalonians*, 489; cf. 494.

### When Is Jesus's Return?

Dedicated chapters of systematic textbooks and many other specialist studies of eschatological matters exist. Our focus here is to summarize what the Thessalonian letters contribute, not to provide a full biblical-theological accounting of Christian eschatology. I structure our findings under some popular questions and headings, noting that Thessalonians does not always contribute as much as our existing eschatological frameworks may hope or expect.

*A Guaranteed Return*

While there are many details that the letters may not flesh out to our satisfaction, they certainly affirm Jesus's return. From a Christian perspective, his return is a dramatic landmark in world history.

So it is theologically significant how reliant we are on Thessalonians for our language. The key term *parousia* is not the only New Testament word used for Jesus's return. But more than a third of its uses for Jesus's return appear here in the Thessalonian letters (and only once elsewhere in Paul's writings, 1 Cor. 15:23). The six occurrences in our eight chapters far outstrip a handful of other mentions spread between Matthew, James, 2 Peter, and 1 John. Where *parousia* occurs in a church tradition's vocabulary, it's quite likely reliant on Thessalonians.

More important than statistics, we have seen that much of the apostles' teaching in Thessalonians is grounded in the certainty of this parousia. It is confidence in Jesus's return and everything it entails that spurs the apostles and their congregation to persevere in the meantime.

*Miscalculated Timings*

We like to think that believers take Jesus and the New Testament authors at their word. But history is littered with groups who have attempted to nail down the timing of Jesus's return. Even if the day and hour are unknown (Matt. 24:36; 25:13), some have "deduced" the month and year.

Thessalonians affirms Jesus's direct warning that we cannot know when he will return. The clearest imagery is the unpredictable surprise of a thief in the night (1 Thess. 5:2, 4; cf. Matt. 24:43; Luke 12:39;

2 Pet. 3:10; Rev. 3:3; 16:15). Our authors add the helpful imagery of a pregnant woman going into labor: labor is a culmination that's fully expected but whose timing remains unknown (1 Thess. 5:3).

### Other Portents?

Some enthusiasts might protest that the onset of labor can be gauged by additional factors. That almost certainly overinterprets the letter's metaphor. Yes, Jesus himself catalogues various precursors (e.g., "wars and rumors of wars"), but his context clearly insists that these are forerunners: "The end is not yet" (Matt. 24:6; Mark 13:5–8). Yes, these affirm that the end is coming, but they contribute nothing to the knowledge of its timing. Using a different angle on the birthing metaphor, Jesus compares these precursors to labor pains: they confirm that the baby is coming, but one cannot predict the length of labor before the baby arrives.

Some church traditions posit a specific "great tribulation" immediately before Jesus arrives (cf. Matt. 24:21; Rev. 7:14). Some even claim to know the duration of that period, so they attempt to pinpoint its beginning—another attempt to calculate its end date.

I am personally cautious about too simplistic or calculated an approach to such a tribulation. Various biblical phrases could just as readily speak of specific trouble leading to the fall of Jerusalem in AD 70 (not least for Jews) and to general troubles throughout the church age (especially for Christians; cf. 68n13). So 2 Thessalonians 2:3–10 deserves attention when it does suggest an intensification. After the current foretastes of lawlessness, Paul and Silvanus and Timothy forecast "the rebellion" and the public acts of "the man of lawlessness": his coming and revelation, his self-aggrandizement, and his deception of the perishing before he himself is killed. Our authors' brevity is indeed maddening.

Again, caution is required. End-times watchers of all eras have typically determined that things are worse for them than for previous generations. So any intensification is difficult to measure. Nor is there anything here that confirms how the man of lawlessness will be recognized, nor how quickly after his arrival. Nor are we told how long he will operate before Jesus arrives to terminate his malevolence; their two comings are narrated in the same sentence. We have to rely on other Bible passages—themselves scant and imprecise—for any sense of identifying features and their timing. Craig Keener is probably correct that we can recognize the climax of rebellion and suffering and the last of many antichrist figures (see 1 John 2:18) only once Jesus arrives to discontinue them.[15]

We must thus acknowledge the tension between the two Thessalonian letters. It is this tension that can drive some interpreters to deny that the letters are composed by the same team of contributors. But it is a tension found elsewhere in the Bible's eschatology, and it is well captured in the summary titles Craig Blomberg gives: "1 Thessalonians: Christ Is Coming Soon"; "2 Thessalonians: But Not That Soon!"[16]

## What Happens at Jesus's Return?

We have frequently noted that the writers to the Thessalonians give only some of the puzzle pieces. Thessalonians does not present a complete picture. Neither do other parts of Scripture. What do our letters contribute to a fuller biblical eschatology?

### An Unmissable Return

One of the theological shortcomings of popular dispensationalist eschatology is an extra coming of Jesus. His first advent at Christmas is followed by *two* second comings! Coming 2a is alleged to be a secret arrival to rapture believers, while 2b involves the more public parousia, the day of the Lord, final judgment, and so on.

We observed that Jesus's return will not pass unnoticed. The first letter gives three descriptions of loud audio accompaniment: "a cry of command," "the voice of an archangel," and "the sound of the trumpet of God" (1 Thess. 4:16; cf. Matt. 24:31; 1 Cor. 15:52). And the second letter

15 Craig S. Keener, *Revelation*, NIVAC (Grand Rapids, MI: Zondervan, 2000), 360; cf. Wayne A. Grudem, *Systematic Theology: An Introduction to Biblical Doctrine*, 2nd ed. (Grand Rapids, MI: Zondervan Academic, 2020), 1357–58.
16 Craig L. Blomberg and Darlene M. Seal, *From Pentecost to Patmos: An Introduction to Acts through Revelation*, 2nd ed. (London: Apollos, 2021), 203, 219. On the broader balancing of eschatological passages, see, e.g., Grudem, *Systematic Theology*, 1347–59.

assures the Thessalonians that the day of the Lord won't pass unawares (e.g., 2 Thess. 2:1–4). Gordon Fee notes how " 'the manifestation of his coming' [in 2 Thess. 2:8] . . . is intended to emphasize not just the *fact* of his coming, but especially its unmistakable and *evidential* character. . . . Christ's Parousia will be openly manifest to all."[17] Thessalonians says nothing of a secret second coming.

## *A Rapture Unlikely*

Despite its popularity in the last century, there is no evidence of a rapture either, certainly not in the sense of believers being whisked into heaven before a period of intense tribulation suffered by those left behind. This is significant because 1 Thessalonians 4:17 is the only verse in the New Testament to hint at the idea and because it's the verse that dispensationalists identify as central to the doctrine. English Bibles talk here about being "caught up" (for which the old Latin translation used the verb *rapio*). We have seen that the passage tells us nothing about which direction believers travel after meeting Jesus in the air—and that its sense more likely is that the august gathering returns to earth rather than to heaven.

We also recall the pastoral thrust of the passage. Believers who die before Jesus returns will not miss out. They will have a distinguished position in his vanguard. The apostles are equally clear that all believers will thus be with the Lord forever (1 Thess. 4:17; 5:10; 2 Thess. 2:1). These ideas are far more prominent—in 1 Thessalonians 4, in the two Thessalonian letters, and throughout the Bible—than any alleged exempting of living believers from universal difficulties.[18]

## *Judgment and the End of Evil*

Rather than being exempted from tribulation, the Thessalonian letters remind believers that they *do* face difficulties—and regularly—espe-

---

17   Fee, *Thessalonians*, 292.

18   Thus the careful subtitle and content of Michael L. Brown and Craig S. Keener, *Not Afraid of the Antichrist: Why We Don't Believe in a Pre-Tribulation Rapture* (Bloomington, MN: Chosen, 2019). For an analysis of hermeneutical factors from a Thessalonian perspective, see Johnson, *1 and 2 Thessalonians*, 288–305.

cially for joining the Christian journey. Along with the church planters, the Thessalonians have been oppressed since their conversion (1 Thess. 1:6; 2:2, 13–16). Indeed, they've been instructed that afflictions are inevitable (3:3–4; cf. 68n13). And this will remain their experience until Jesus returns and brings evil to naught (2 Thess. 1:3–8).

These letters offer little detail about how the forces of evil are vanquished. The ease with which Jesus dismisses the man of lawlessness leads many to conclude that, as far as our authors want their readers to care, "there is no great final battle between human forces called Armageddon, only a final divine execution."[19] We note too that God the Father exacts justice alongside God the Son (e.g., 2 Thess. 1:5–8). They work together in final salvation as much as in initial salvation.

Just as my book has been tracing the journey of Christian believers, some scholars see Thessalonians mapping the journey of unbelievers, a journey that culminates in condemnation (cf. Rom. 1:18–32; James 1:14–15).[20] Unrepentant humans are judged alongside the forces of evil (2 Thess. 1:5–10; 2:9–12). Only the briefest glimpse of their fate is provided: "They will suffer the punishment of eternal destruction, away from the presence of the Lord and from the glory of his might" (1:9). So, for example, we must look to other passages to consider what this suffering entails (e.g., Matt. 10:28; Luke 16:19–31) or to confirm that rebels' eternal absence from the Lord's presence is experienced consciously (e.g., Rev. 14:9–11).

## Salvation Completed

The same balance holds true for those reaching the positive end of the journey of salvation. Thessalonians confirms that believers remain forever with the Lord. But the location and circumstances of that blessed condition are assumed rather than articulated.

---

19  Witherington, *1 and 2 Thessalonians*, 222; cf. Gupta, *1–2 Thessalonians*, 138; Ernest Best, *The First and Second Epistles to the Thessalonians*, BNTC (London: A&C Black, 1972), 304. The same sentiment is often touted for Rev. 19:11–21.

20  I. Howard Marshall, *1 and 2 Thessalonians*, NCB (London: Marshall, Morgan & Scott, 1983), 204; Witherington, *1 and 2 Thessalonians*, 224–25; both draw on J. B. Lightfoot.

Recalling the "tenses" of salvation, we see that salvation is completed only when God's final favorable judgment is rendered. Douglas Moo's summary of Pauline theology observes that "salvation covers the entirety of Christian experience." He reminds us that salvation language is used of God's past, present, and future work in our salvific journey, and he calculates that the Pauline writings most frequently address God's rescue in the *final* steps of our course.[21] Already this future focus of rescue from wrath is the climax of the opening Thessalonian chapter (1 Thess. 1:10), and it rounds out the extended specific instructions in that same letter (5:9–10). Both letters' regular eschatological emphases keep these final steps in view.

This remains a useful challenge for us. Many church traditions focus on the *past* tense of salvation: on God's decision—and often on ours—made in our past that we follow Jesus. Our prior chapter drew attention to God's *ongoing* work of salvific transformation, making us increasingly suited for his presence. And now Moo assures us that Paul's own emphases are fixed primarily on the *end* of the journey. We misrepresent the Bible's teaching if we focus on one tense to the exclusion of the others. We may well also dishearten those under way on the journey if we miscommunicate the various teachings that flag the start of the course, its end, and evidence of progress along the way.

### Holding on to Hope

We conclude with a reminder that the Thessalonian letters emphasize eschatology not for intellectual gratification but for pastoral care. The Corinthian congregation especially lacked love, so we hear "love" foregrounded ahead of "faith" and "hope" (1 Cor. 13:13). The Thessalonian believers are generally loving well, so "hope" is given much of the spotlight as they await Jesus's return.[22]

---

21   Douglas J. Moo, *A Theology of Paul and His Letters: The Gift of the New Realm in Christ*, BTNT (Grand Rapids, MI: Zondervan Academic, 2021), 468.

22   Raymond F. Collins, *First Corinthians*, SP 7 (Collegeville, MN: Liturgical Press, 1999), 484–85.

Thus various mentions of judgment and the rebellion and the man of lawlessness are not meant merely to further the Thessalonians' intellectual progress. Nor are they warnings addressed to those responding poorly to the gospel. They are not focused on a particular eschatological timeline or even, in this instance, foregrounding Jesus's power. No, the summary details are to encourage the afflicted *believers* to persist in their journey, confident that their current troublesome circumstances are for a limited time only.[23]

The description just given is especially visible in 2 Thessalonians 1–2, but it can be applied to each of the eschatological encouragements spaced across both letters. Each discussion of God's plans for the future is deployed to motivate the Thessalonians in their faithful persistence *now*, living and growing in holiness in preparation for eternity in the presence of the holy Trinity. Our coming chapters turn to consider further the shape of ministry and doctrine for the present.

---

23 "Eschatology thus becomes a pastoral tool to encourage these beleaguered believers." Nijay K. Gupta, "Thessalonians, Letters to the," *DPL*[2] 1053.

# 4

# Delighted to Share Our Lives as Well

## The Ministries of Leaders and Church Members

GOOD MINISTRIES AIM to replicate. This agreeable statement is hard to defend from the Thessalonian letters, especially when the impression may be that the congregation isn't widely engaged in evangelism and seems instructed to keep a low profile. A study of church leadership is also difficult when Paul and Silvanus and Timothy are church founders—and now at a distance—rather than local congregational leaders on the ground. The Thessalonian letters contain no direct address to leaders as we find to individual apostolic delegates in the letters to Timothy and Titus, to overseers and deacons in Philippians, or to elders in 1 Peter 5.

Still, as in most New Testament letters, the apostles relate sufficient autobiographical content that it is viable to consider what Thessalonians contributes to the overall picture. We must be alert that the apostles distinguish themselves from local church leaders, who are mentioned only in passing (1 Thess. 5:12–13). So what we learn is more immediately applicable to apostolic ministries, perhaps in a church-planting sense, than to longer-term local shepherding. Of course, the two roles overlap, yet we must not too conveniently conflate them. A corresponding caution is that the letters do not seek to provide overt instructions on congregational leadership. Again, we are reading letters *from* leaders and somewhat *about* leaders, but these are not letters *to* leaders.

We are ultimately driven to this secondhand, indirect investigation of leadership because (1) the New Testament provides less detail than we may desire and (2) the passages that include any detail are written later in the life of the first-century church. We join Derek Tidball's lament that "it is impossible to say much with any certainty about local leadership in these early Pauline churches because so little is said in Paul's letters."[1]

With such caveats in place, this chapter outlines what we can learn from Thessalonians about the status, the character, and the activities of church planters and leaders. This gives rise to a fourth section, in which we discern some responsibilities of church members toward each other.

### The Status of Leaders

These "glass half empty" caveats open this chapter because they apply immediately to issues of status. Regular local leaders carry a degree of status, which our letters hint at. But the leadership authority most firmly on display in Thessalonians concerns the apostolic authors. Such apostolic authority does not obviously apply to local pastors in either the first or twenty-first century.

That said, our letters extend the term "apostle" to include Silvanus and Timothy (1 Thess. 2:6/7), using the term's broader sense of "teacher" or "missionary" (see 9n10, in the introduction). So the Thessalonian letters show that it is appropriate to consider how believers and contemporary leaders might emulate the three church planters ("how you ought to imitate *us*," 2 Thess. 3:7). While we rightly take care in considering what parallels exist between the original biblical context and our day, we can still be confident in imitating biblical role models. In Thessalonians, that is especially the case where modern ministry resembles and overlaps with that of these authors, such as in planting and nurturing congregations of God's people.

---

1    Derek Tidball, *Ministry by the Book: New Testament Patterns for Pastoral Leadership* (Downers Grove, IL: IVP Academic, 2008), 125.

*Leaders as Equals*

Although we shortly consider the authority that these apostolic figures might exercise, the Thessalonian letters foreground a servanthood view of ministry, perhaps more so than any other correspondence associated with Paul. The dominant imagery is of senior family members who lovingly and sacrificially care for other members—a far cry from despots lording it over subjugated minions.

Family imagery abounds. We have already observed in chapter 1 the startling barrage of "brothers and sisters" terminology (ESV mg.). Our authors make every effort to consolidate this relationship, mentioning it (on average) once every five verses!

We know this is more than some sterile or stereotypical Christian greeting, because such sibling language is supplemented by several other family images. The list is tidily compiled in the title of Trevor Burke's survey, which furnishes a useful checklist for the following summary: "Mother, Father, Infant, Orphan, Brother."[2]

It is not uncommon for Paul to cast himself as a spiritual father to congregations and individuals, as he does with the Corinthians (1 Cor. 4:14–15), with Timothy and Titus (1 Tim. 1:2; 2 Tim. 1:2; Titus 1:4), and with Onesimus (Philem. 10). He also sometimes invokes maternal imagery, as when he seeks to (re)birth the Galatians (Gal. 4:19). Our apostolic writers happily identify both with motherhood and fatherhood imagery in relation to the Thessalonians (1 Thess. 2:7, 11).[3]

Some might imagine that parental images inherently invoke a degree of authority. The maternal imagery seeks to communicate the apostles'

---

2   Trevor J. Burke, "Mother, Father, Infant, Orphan, Brother: Paul's Variegated Pastoral Strategy towards His Thessalonian Church Family," in *Paul as Pastor*, ed. Brian S. Rosner, Andrew S. Malone, and Trevor J. Burke (London: Bloomsbury T&T Clark, 2018), 123–41.

3   Perhaps the Pauline team shares the Jewish sentiment that "mothers . . . are more sympathetic in their feelings toward their offspring than fathers" (4 Macc. 15:4 NETS). So David A. deSilva, *The Letter to the Galatians*, NICNT (Grand Rapids, MI: Eerdmans, 2018), 386. Among the growing literature on maternal images, see Beverly Roberts Gaventa, *Our Mother Saint Paul* (Louisville: Westminster John Knox, 2007). For a thoughtful balance of authority *and love* from ancient fathers, see Jeffrey A. D. Weima, "Infants, Nursing Mother, and Father: Paul's Portrayal of a Pastor," *CTJ* 37 (2002): 209–29, esp. 224–27.

tender affections and self-sacrificial service (2:7–9) rather than paren-tal influence. The paternal imagery, while hardly domineering, does use terms associated with authority, such as "exhorted," "encouraged," and "charged" (2:10–12). So these familial similes present a mixed picture. On the one hand, the apostles do not disavow their authority, while on the other hand, they are at pains to avoid any unintended overly "authoritarian" inference. They even reverse the family relationship. While Thessalonians is missing any trace of Paul's customary "slave/servant" language (e.g., 1 Cor. 9:19; 2 Cor. 4:5), a key claim reads this way:

> For we never came . . . seeking glory from people, whether from you or from others—though we were able to, by weight of being apostles of Christ—but we came as infants among you. (1 Thess. 2:5–7a, my trans.)

The apostles describe themselves as "infants," and they clearly do so as an image of their voluntary humility.[4] The image of being humble infants, even dependents, continues a few verses later as they lament "having been orphaned from you" (2:17 NASB). They were humble during their time in Thessalonica, and they continue that posture as they now write to their family.

### Leaders with Authority

We should delight in and learn from our authors' self-effacement. The scoreboard in 1 Thessalonians 2 does appear to read two recol-lections of "we were parent-like" balanced against two boasts of "we were childlike," all complemented by the myriad mentions of a sibling relationship. It looks like an even matching, and modern church lead-ers should heed the apostles' balanced approach to the wielding of power. But there remain several hints of seniority, even if the weighty

---

4   Bible translations can be slow in moving from the more entrenched "we were *gentle*" (e.g., CSB, ESV) toward the scholarly consensus, "we were *infants*" (e.g., NIV, NET). At stake in Greek is a single letter.

honorific "apostles" occurs only in the passage just cited and for the purpose of *relinquishing* authoritarian demands and avoiding any imposition. Thessalonians conveys a sense of seniority more subtly than other letters.

Scholars note how our senders haven't used "apostle" language in their opening greetings. The absence is significant, given that almost every other Pauline letter includes this title. Apart from 1 and 2 Thessalonians, it is missing only from letters where Paul (each time with Timothy) is keen to frontload mutual dependence and downplay any authoritative asymmetry (Phil. 1:1; Philem. 1). Of course, in Philemon there are alternative ways to express authority, which are woven through the remainder of the missive. So also in Thessalonians.

Later in this chapter, we consider the importance of imitating leaders. Some interpreters detect in this a subtle flexing of apostolic authority. They see the early recollection that "you became imitators of us" as a gentle reminder of a pecking order (1 Thess. 1:6).[5] Even then it is unclear if this is a claim to a hierarchical priority or merely to a chronological priority: the apostles were earlier converts whom the Thessalonians could emulate, which in this context means imitating their faithful conversion and persistence despite affliction.

The same ambiguity is seen in other passages. At the end of the largely thanksgiving section that fills so much of the first three chapters, the apostles pray to return to the Thessalonians "and supply what is lacking in [their] faith" (3:10). It is clear that the apostles have something the Thessalonians do not and that it is their God-given responsibility to shape the congregation, but they express this without a direct claim to authority.

Such a claim to authority bubbles closer to the surface as the letter moves from retrospective remembrances toward prospective instructions. We have already explored in chapter 2 the detailed instructions and succinct injunctions of 1 Thessalonians 4–5. That lengthy section opens with a variety of rhetorical strategies. English translations of

---

5    Charles A. Wanamaker, *The Epistles to the Thessalonians*, NIGTC (Grand Rapids, MI: Eerdmans, 1990), 81.

4:1–2 struggle to weave these together in a readable fashion, so I simply address the component clauses:

- The same kinds of gentle parental coaxing seen earlier reoccur here: "We ask and urge you" (cf. 2:11–12).
- The content or goal of this encouragement is "how you ought to walk and to please God."
- Assurance is given that the authors are repeating past directives. Indeed, this point is made twice: "we gave" and "you received."
- Assurance is also made that the Thessalonians are already doing well at complying. The call is to continue to walk this way (cf. NASB: "Excel even more").

Each rhetorical element is already noteworthy and has contemporary application for ministry (and we return to rhetoric shortly). My own tendency is to see, so far, an evenhanded giving and taking. I might then wonder if the apostles are downplaying their authoritative rank. But I cannot ignore that a degree of authority does creep in. It's here twice. The apostles intone, "We ask and urge you *in the Lord Jesus,*" recalling "what instructions we gave you *through the Lord Jesus*" (4:1–2).

These two verses join a variety of cajoling throughout the letters. In an age when spiritual authority is too readily misused, I am keen to highlight the many "carrots" employed. Some "sticks" are also waved judiciously. The ensuing call to holiness grounds 1 Thessalonians 4–5 entirely, and it recognizes that such concerns for holiness originate not with these human leaders but with God—and that any disregard for these concerns is thus an affront to the one who demands and facilitates such holiness (4:7–8)! Regular prayers of thanksgiving and request are "the will of God in Christ Jesus" for the believers (5:16–18). And there is a brief moment, recognized as odd by commentators, when Paul himself seems very heavy-handed in what sounds like a simple request: he puts the Thessalonians "under oath before the Lord" that the letter be read out to all the church members (5:27). The same occurs in the second letter, where the commands framing the disruptive nonworkers are given "in the name of our Lord Jesus Christ" (2 Thess. 3:6) and "in the Lord Jesus Christ" (3:12). Throughout both letters the authors express some expectations more forcefully than others. Apostolic authority is not flaunted, but neither is it absent.

We have already suggested that apostolic authority is derived. By definition all senses of the terms "apostle" and "apostolic" acknowledge the authority of a prior sender. God's apostles are commissioned by God to communicate *his* message on his authority. And again, despite a solo use of the word "apostles," our letters show awareness of God's commission. The apostles declare "the gospel/word of God" (esp. 1 Thess. 2:2, 8, 9, 13), and we saw in chapter 1 that such a phrase suggests a message belonging to or emanating from God. Thus, Paul's team seeks to please not those who hear them but the one who commissioned them with this communiqué. This is especially clear in the same Thessalonian chapter that has become much the focus of our current discussion: "Just as we have been *approved by God* to be *entrusted* with the gospel, so we speak, not to please man, but *to please God* who tests our hearts" (2:4). And of course, there are many examples and thanksgivings and petitions addressed to the triune God.

## The Character of Leaders

Discussion of the apostles' authority merges with the character traits they exhibit. It is almost artificial to add a fresh heading here, for the character of leaders continues seamlessly as we consider the attitude with which they discharge their authority.

We have just discovered that church leadership involves navigating a three-way dance. In local ministry, my father would sometimes quip, "I am a servant of the church, but the church is not my master." That same sentiment is clear in Thessalonians. With a message and a ministry authorized by God, our apostles strive to show their accountability to him even as they serve the church. As much as they hold themselves up for the Thessalonians' critique, they also invoke God as witness to the selfless execution of their commission (1 Thess. 2:5, 10). It is encouraging, and perhaps surprising or confronting, to observe such persistent claims of divine accountability and clear conscience of a commission acquitted well (e.g., Acts 23:1; 24:16; Rom. 1:9; 9:1; 1 Cor. 4:4; 2 Cor. 1:12, 23; 2:17; 12:19; Gal. 1:20; Phil. 1:8; 2 Tim. 1:3). The same accountability and clear conscience are expressly expected of the apostles' vocational successors as well (e.g., 1 Tim. 1:3–7, 18–19; 3:9; Heb. 13:18).

Some of us are prone to a hasty binary focusing on pleasing God at the expense of pleasing humans. The clauses of 1 Thessalonians 2:4–6 could be read this way, as can other verses such as Romans 12:1–2 or Galatians 1:10. But it's also important to acknowledge Scripture's interest in all three parties in the "dance." The bigger New Testament picture is for God's leaders to *also* please people—provided, of course, that this is in tune with serving God (e.g., Matt. 5:14–16; Rom. 12:17–18; 1 Cor. 10:31–33; 2 Cor. 8:21; Titus 2:1–10; 3:1–2; 1 Pet. 2:12). We have already seen our letters' concerns that the church retain a good standing with members of the wider community.

Serving a personal God, whether as church planters or local leaders or congregants, brooks the logical and theological possibility of *displeasing* God. We catch a glimpse of this possibility at the end of the section we have focused on. The apostolic team has commended their own ministry as a way of assuring the Thessalonians of the validity of the gospel message they've embraced—and for which they continue to suffer (1 Thess. 2:1–12). The ensuing verse then reinforces the gravity of the Christian God and his gospel message:

> This is why we constantly thank God, because when you received the word of God that you heard from us, you welcomed it not as a human message, but as it truly is, the word of God, which also works effectively in you who believe. (1 Thess. 2:13 CSB)

In turn, the Thessalonians are assured that they have done the right thing *even though* they are suffering for it. They have admirably imitated other "churches of God in Christ Jesus," in this case especially those churches in Judea (2:14). The Thessalonians are suffering from their

Greek compatriots the same opposition that the Judean churches suffered from the Jews. The ESV margin note reminds us that "the Jews" should be interpreted thoughtfully, but the thrust of the verses is clear. Gentile unbelievers are harassing Gentile believers in the same way that Jewish unbelievers have harassed Jewish believers. In both spheres, and (in this illustration) particularly in parts of Judea, such people "displease God and are hostile to everyone" (2:15 CSB, NIV). Note how such hostility is measured here: it is especially expressed through opposing the spread of the Christian gospel and the salvation it offers to God's wider world. It is possible to stand against God and his saving message and thus to incur his wrath.

We have previously seen these same emphases reprised in the second letter. Much of 2 Thessalonians 1 is an assurance that the church's afflictions are not some indicator of God's plans going awry; rather, they are on the right track (esp. 1:4, 5). And we hear a catalogue of those who incur God's judgment as those who "do not obey the gospel of our Lord Jesus," who are deceived into perishing, who "refused to love the truth and so be saved . . . but had pleasure in unrighteousness" (1:8; 2:10, 12; cf. 3:2).

Our authors are thus concerned, like gentle parents, to flag for their spiritual family the behaviors that both please and displease God. Obviously, they nurture the former and denounce the latter. We have noticed the pleasant surprise that it is to see so much positive encouragement; in many places the Thessalonians are inveigled directly and indirectly to continue in the right direction (e.g., 1 Thess. 1:2–3; 3:8–9, 12; 4:1, 9–10; 5:11; 2 Thess. 1:3–4; 2:15; 3:4, 13). Yet we have also noted other passages in which parental warnings are offered against real or potential deviations (esp. 1 Thess. 4:1–12).[6]

Our apostolic leaders are thus coordinating this three-way dance. They are under God's authority and striving to please him. Their Thessalonian flock is likewise under God's authority and encouraged to

---

6 On this latter passage, Gary Shogren particularly urges proactive pastoring. Those inadvertently or wantonly straying from holiness won't be *inviting* correction. *1 & 2 Thessalonians*, ZECNT 13 (Grand Rapids, MI: Zondervan, 2012), 174–75.

keep pleasing him. And the apostles' authority to plant and direct the church can be perceived at multiple levels. (1) Paul and Silvanus and Timothy were Christian believers before the Thessalonians; they are like older siblings in a family. (2) They founded and nurtured the church in Thessalonica; they are like parents directing a family. (3) And they did so at the behest of God, who entrusted them with a message and evaluates their performance.

We modern interpreters are likely to gravitate more toward one of these levels than the others, based on our preferences for authority. Those who favor a congregational polity will be warmed by the evenhanded shepherding offered by (elder) siblings. Those who expect up-front directive leadership will appreciate the (gentle) flexing of authoritative muscle. We all benefit from the range of imagery that the Thessalonian letters tender, including the alternate examples that we may not naturally incline to.

Finally, we must acknowledge that there is not a one-to-one correspondence between these apostolic writers and local church leadership. The model that Paul and Silvanus and Timothy offer may be, at best, a starting point that needs to be adapted rather than adopted wholesale. While we can definitely learn from their example, we should allow that local pastoral leadership today might not be an exact carbon copy of what we've read about the missionaries to Thessalonica.

Of course, we wish that the letters said more about local church leadership than the little we glimpse in 1 Thessalonians 5:12–13. It is unclear if the local leaders serve in formally appointed roles or are singled out as zealous volunteers. We can see *that* they are described as those "who labor among you," so we can clearly speak of "workers" serving the congregation. There is genuine debate among commentators as to *what* they do "in the Lord": Do they hold leadership authority (ESV, NASB, NRSV), or do they care for the flock (NIV; cf. CSB mg.)? The word at stake can emphasize either the authoritative basis of their labors or the mutual benefits thereof, and fair arguments are raised in favor of each alternative. At least what commentators agree on is that (1) these church workers are distinguished within the congregation: not every member is being honored in these verses; and (2) these workers are identified more in terms of their behavior than on the basis of some titled position. If they carry some kind of formalized authority, then they are to be respected and esteemed not for their office but for their service therein, laboring on behalf of the congregation just as the apostles had (cf. 3:5), and for exemplifying the love-induced labor and the admonishing concern exhorted of all the Thessalonian believers (1:3; 5:14). Conversely, if these are "merely" volunteer workers—perhaps capable benefactors—whose initiative or resources see them contributing more than other church members, again it is their faithful service rather than their societal position that earns praise.

In turn, the precise instructions here are to the rest of the church. Fortuitously, they apply across different models of contemporary church leadership. Congregants are to respect and esteem those who serve the church, whether such servants are formally appointed or are volunteer activists. The work of these servants is general enough to apply to a range of contributions, although "laboring" and "admonishing" certainly resemble something of the apostles' past and present ministries toward the congregation. We might even suggest that these two verbs identify both actions and words. The apostles elsewhere pray concerning both, commending to God the Thessalonians' "every good work and word" (2 Thess. 2:17). And the leaders of another first-century congregation are to be imitated because of both their speaking and their way of life (Heb. 13:7).

## The Work of Leaders

We have already surveyed much of what the apostles describe of their church-planting ministry. We have also glimpsed the briefest snippet that Thessalonians contributes to the broader picture: that the first-century church singled out some members of congregations for their special efforts. We might zero in on a few specific goals for leaders that our letters suggest.

## God's Undershepherds

The language of "pastors" is absent from Thessalonians and, indeed, is rarely associated with Paul (only Acts 20:28–29; Eph. 4:11). Jesus is the supreme pastor who shepherds God's flock, an image more recurrent than we might initially guess (Matt. 2:6; John 10:11–16; Heb. 13:20; 1 Pet. 2:25; 5:4; Rev. 7:17). Of course, this image develops notions tracing back into the Old Testament, where God weighs the better and worse shepherds of his flock and plans to supersede them (esp. Ezek. 34).

Still, it is a fortuitous word, especially for church traditions that label their workers "pastors." It conjures up the language of animal shepherds—from which "pastor" is derived—and their active participation in a flock's well-being. We recall David's concern to protect his animal flocks from predators (1 Sam. 17:34–36), just as congregational pastors shield their human flocks (Acts 20:28–31), as did Jesus himself (John 10:11). We recall Jacob's work to maintain and extend his master's herds, even at cost to his own progress (Gen. 30:27–30; 31:38–39; although God ultimately redirected Laban's prosperity to Jacob). While the Thessalonian letters do not invoke such shepherding imagery, they thoroughly endorse the same concerns: to see a flock grow to full maturity, if not also to multiply in size (cf. Col. 1:28–29).

## God's Communicators

One of a spiritual shepherd's opportunities to "feed" the flock is with God's words and instructions.[7] We have earlier highlighted the persistent language of "word" and "gospel" in the letters, as well as the happy recounting of "the dual theme of the apostles' faithful preaching of God's word and the Thessalonians' faithful reception of it."[8]

---

7   So the title and emphases of Allan Chapple, "Paul's Ministry of the Word according to 1 Thessalonians," in *Serving God's Words: Windows on Preaching and Ministry*, ed. Paul A. Barker, Richard J. Condie, and Andrew S. Malone (Nottingham, UK: Inter-Varsity Press, 2011), 85–100.

8   Douglas J. Moo, *A Theology of Paul and His Letters: The Gift of the New Realm in Christ*, BTNT (Grand Rapids, MI: Zondervan Academic, 2021), 91. Seyoon Kim especially promotes a strong link between the delivery and reception of the gospel message, finding this interplay the primary structure of 1 Thess. 1–3; most recently, Seyoon Kim and F. F.

Nor is it only a narrow, direct commission that the apostles proclaim. Allan Chapple joins others in observing just how much of the content of 1 and 2 Thessalonians reflects what will eventually be codified in the written Gospels, especially Matthew's.[9] Other books of the New Testament are laden with more obvious citations of and allusions to the Old Testament, so the Thessalonian letters may appear innocuously as brand-new new covenant missives. Yet there are gentle hints of Old Testament ideas and even Old Testament language when we scratch the surface.[10] Our apostles have done their biblical homework, even if they choose not to cite chapter and verse to this particular congregation.

## Effective and Affective Communicators

It is somewhat unclear whether the apostles include such biblical material consciously. Perhaps their lives and ministries are simply marinated in the stories of the Old Testament and what will become the New Testament. Or perhaps their writings reflect what they have shared with the Thessalonians in person, and they expect their Thessalonian readers to catch their allusive reminders.

We certainly find other hints that God's apostles are careful communicators. They exercise relevant gifts of local rhetoric to accomplish their ministry goals. We have already spotted (in chap. 2) some of the rhetorical skills on display in 1 Thessalonians 4:1–2. There and elsewhere they employ standard formulas to reinforce right practices and right doctrines. These remind the Thessalonians of what they *do* know or what they *should* know, formulas such as "you know" or "remember" or "you are witnesses" (e.g., 1 Thess. 1:5; 2:1–2, 5, 9–12; 3:3–4; 4:2, 6, 11; 5:1–2; 2 Thess. 2:5–6; 3:6, 7, 10). Such formulas appealing to past experience occur occasionally in Paul's other letters (1 Cor. 12:2; 16:15;

---

Bruce, *1 & 2 Thessalonians*, 2nd ed., WBC 45 (Grand Rapids, MI: Zondervan Academic, 2023). Kim shares my caution against reading these chapters as intentional exemplars for local leaders or readers.

9   Chapple, "Paul's Ministry of the Word," 95–96.

10  Along with commentaries, see Jeffrey A. D. Weima, "1–2 Thessalonians," in *Commentary on the New Testament Use of the Old Testament*, ed. G. K. Beale and D. A. Carson (Grand Rapids, MI: Baker Academic, 2007), 871–89.

Gal. 4:13; Phil. 4:15; 2 Tim. 1:15; 3:14–15), but their prominence here in Thessalonians underscores this useful communication tool.[11]

Other rhetorical flourishes may not employ particular key terms, and they may even be all but invisible to us because of their common sense. Our apostles regularly rehearse the believers' past and present good behaviors (esp. 1 Thess. 1:6–10; 2:13–14; 4:1–2, 9–10; 5:11; 2 Thess. 2:13–15; 3:4). Thus sometimes directly but more often indirectly, they reinforce continuation of such conduct. The same occurs with autobiographical reports of the apostles' own behaviors: calling to mind events that cast them and their authority in a good light (esp. 1 Thess. 2:1–12; 2 Thess. 3:6–10). It is little surprise that we find other examples of self-revelation. Especially in 1 Thessalonians 2:17–3:10, the apostolic collaborators—and here especially Paul himself—put their emotions on display to communicate concern in order to maintain favorable contact and elicit a favorable response.

Those of us who focus on straight talk may miss or dismiss the apostles' use of thoughtful language. We may be unaccustomed to pondering how they employ such language to shape their congregation's responses. So it is a challenge for us as we interpret how these preachers and authors harness the effective communication tools of their day to serve their ministry.[12] Straight talkers may miss features such as the use of irony, as when Paul uses careful and clear language to explain how he opted to avoid dazzling the Corinthians with sparkly words (1 Cor. 2:1–5) or when the preacher to the Hebrews announces that he's running too short on time to detail what he then spends another six verses on (Heb. 11:32–38). So we might likewise misread phrases such as those in 1 Thessalonians 2:5 and infer that there are no rhetorical tricks in the apostles' speech or writings. Yet it is plausibly suggested that 2:1–12, the very passage that presents the apostles' humility and

---

11  In turn, other letters include alternative tools to consider. Thus Romans and Corinthians employ the corresponding negative challenge: "Do you *not* know?" (e.g., Rom. 6:16; 11:2; 1 Cor. 3:16; 5:6; 6:2–3, 9, 15–19; 9:13, 24).

12  See the survey of Marion Carson, "For Now We Live: A Study of Paul's Pastoral Leadership in 1 Thessalonians," *Themelios* 30, no. 3 (2005): 23–41.

disinterest in human praise, is in fact a judicious example of gently *seeking* the goodwill of the audience! (The philosopher Plutarch [ca. AD 46–120] would shortly codify the ground rules in an aptly titled work, *On Inoffensive Self-Praise*.) The ensuing autobiographical account in 2:17–3:10 is similarly designed not only to narrate emotions but also to tug on heartstrings.[13]

Some might worry that such features sound too humanistic and unfitting for Christian Scripture. But we find that divine inspiration regularly incorporates the rhetorical tools of communication, which are evident in all Paul's writings. They are still active in his final canonical letter, which starts with an impassioned account of mutual longing and ends with Paul rhetorically urging his protégé Timothy to a hasty reunion (2 Tim. 1:3–4; 4:9–21).

We have already noted how the apostles make use of Old Testament ideas and language, even if in these particular letters they don't use direct quotations and formal introductions like "As the prophet says . . ." or "As Moses writes . . ." They may likewise slip other communication strategies under our radars. When our authors speak of the dead as "asleep" (1 Thess. 4:13–15), is this a Christian euphemism for temporary rest or a Greco-Roman illustration of apparently permanent death? Are our authors carefully accommodating both? They shortly paint the wider world as being surprised when Jesus returns, focused instead on the comforts of "peace and security" (5:3). Scholars debate whether this was a contemporary Roman motto, an allusion to past slogans from Israel's prophets, or a hypothetical sentiment characterizing unbelievers' self-centeredness (cf. Matt. 24:36–51). We receive and comprehend and replicate such terms differently depending on their origin and intent, but regardless, they illustrate clever communication.

---

13  Most commentators keep watch over rhetorical matters, not least the "socio rhetorical commentary" of Ben Witherington III, *1 and 2 Thessalonians: A Socio-Rhetorical Commentary* (Grand Rapids, MI: Eerdmans, 2006). See 20–36 for an introductory sample of his concerns. Although Witherington is not convinced, other scholars continue to see Thessalonians (especially the first epistle) as containing substantial elements of a "friendship letter"; e.g., David A. deSilva, *An Introduction to the New Testament: Contexts, Methods, and Ministry Formation*, 2nd ed. (Downers Grove, IL: IVP Academic, 2018), 467–68.

Ultimately, we should be humbled and challenged by such insights. They call us to be ever more alert to the effective communication strategies of the first century. We need to realize that simple phrases may be doing far more than we immediately recognize. And they invite us to consider what twenty-first-century strategies we ourselves use. As commentators sometimes paraphrase, are we aware of the strategies or ironies, or even outright confusions—when we intone, "I won't mention . . . ," or, "You don't need to be told . . ."?

## Mute Models

Evangelicals are rightly uncomfortable with the apocryphal adage attributed to Francis of Assisi "Preach the gospel at all times; if necessary, use words." Certainly, our Thessalonian authors have had much to say about their past and present word-focused preaching, teaching, and writing! Yet they readily affirm that word-based ministry is helpfully supplemented by a corresponding lifestyle. We have already studied the behaviors expected of believers, including the impact on unbelievers.

This also invites us to observe the apostles' interest in imitation. Paul offers the most complete articulation elsewhere: "Be imitators of me, as I am of Christ" (1 Cor. 11:1). There are occasional glimpses of either part of this instruction throughout the New Testament (1 Cor. 4:16; Gal. 4:12; Eph. 5:1; Phil. 3:17; 4:9; cf. Heb. 6:12; 12:2, 3; 13:7; 1 Pet. 2:21; 3 John 11). Again, however, our Thessalonian letters "punch above their weight" with multiple overt references to imitation.

The opening thanksgiving praises God, and indirectly the Thessalonians, because they "became imitators" of the apostles and of the Lord Jesus, not least in joining God's journey in the face of opposition (1 Thess. 1:6). That same praise for imitative persistence continues when the thanksgiving is reprised shortly thereafter; the Thessalonians are enduring like the persecuted churches of Judea and like Jesus (2:14–15). When the second letter raises the importance of manual labor so as to preserve the reputation of the gospel, the apostles twice point back to their own intentional example (2 Thess. 3:6–8, 9–10); each time the apostolic prototype is put on display to reinforce verbal instructions.

In turn, the apostles praise the Thessalonians for the aspects of their behavior that are positive examples to others. The key passage comes at the end of the opening chapter (1 Thess. 1:6–10). One measure of the Thessalonians' thorough conversion is that they "became an example to all the believers in Macedonia and in Achaia" (1:7). The nature of this example is fleshed out in the next two (somewhat parallel) clauses: "The word of the Lord sounded forth from you" in both northern and southern Greece, and "your faith in God has gone forth everywhere" (1:8). Believers throughout the region, if not also further afield, have caught wind of the Thessalonians' conversion as expressed in their faithful worship of God and patient waiting for Jesus's return! (We saw in chap. 2 of this book the possibility that the Thessalonians have even become model evangelists. Many commentators favor such an interpretation, and I would love it to prove true. But the text seems to focus more on the impact of the Thessalonians' reputation on other believers.)[14] Even in subsequent letters the apostles can report how they boast of the Thessalonian church to other congregations (2 Thess. 1:4; cf. 2 Cor. 8:1–5). Leon Morris observes that this is the only Pauline church expressly named as a "model."[15]

Of course, other congregations are praised for good behavior and for imitation. Individual apostles and other church leaders are also praised and instructed as models (Acts 20:31–35; 1 Tim. 1:16; 4:12; Titus 2:7–8; 1 Pet. 5:2–3). But it is the Thessalonian letters that most clearly and most densely narrate the sequence. The Lord Jesus sets an example for the apostles, whom churches then imitate, even becoming models themselves for subsequent believers.

### Every-Member Ministry

In exploring leadership, we have noted the natural tendency toward confirmation bias. We may well judge the Thessalonian letters to emphasize the congregational models we prefer.

---

14   Timothy A. Brookins, *First and Second Thessalonians*, Paideia (Grand Rapids, MI: Baker Academic, 2021), 35; cf. Wanamaker, *Thessalonians*, 83.

15   Leon Morris, *The First and Second Epistles to the Thessalonians*, rev. ed., NICNT (Grand Rapids, MI: Eerdmans, 1991), 49–50.

Our illustration of a three-way dance probably should add another participant. Our letters seem to suggest that God (with Jesus) leads his church, communicates through his apostles, *governs via another layer of local leaders (possibly elders)*, and is received and obeyed by the church's members. This intermediate layer is all but invisible in 1 and 2 Thessalonians, so it is easy to "choose our own adventure" here. We might conflate local leaders with the apostles and assume their ministries to be nearly identical. We might interpolate our favorite leadership model and merely assume how the Thessalonian church operated. Or we might ignore altogether the possibility or authority of local leaders.

So I am likewise alert to the pitfalls of discussing and promoting the place of every-member ministry, especially when I myself am keenly in favor of it. Yet these letters do lean toward concurring with other, better-detailed epistles on this score, and we cannot leave the phenomenon unmentioned. Without disregarding the place of local leaders, other Pauline epistles famously depict the church as Christ's body with each member contributing (Rom. 12:3–8; 1 Cor. 12; cf. 1 Pet. 4:10–11). So we can appreciate Gary Shogren's verdict on 1 Thessalonians: "While Paul implies the existence of church leaders (5:12–13), they are by no means the primary focus of the church's ministry, which is carried out by the congregation."[16]

What does the congregation's ministry look like?

In the one glimpse of more senior leaders, the congregation is called to respect and esteem such leaders (5:12–13). It is also plausible that the final command in these verses calls for peaceable living as much for the leaders' respite as for the congregation's (cf. Heb. 13:17). We might then imagine that the following succinct instructions are echoed and modeled by the leaders, but the instructions are formally directed to all the church's "brothers and sisters" (ESV mg.). Thus the church family as a whole is responsible for nurturing and guiding those who are flagging in the journey, for encouraging good behavior and thankful praying, for permitting and testing Spirit-fueled prophecies, for

---

16  Shogren, *1 & 2 Thessalonians*, 350.

praying for the apostles, and for generally greeting and maintaining congregational fellowship (1 Thess. 5:14–22, 25–27; 2 Thess. 3:1, 6–15).

Two key expectations are especially promoted in our letters. The church's members already *love* each other—an attitude lauded as "taught by God" (1 Thess. 4:9)—and several apostolic prayers praise such behavior and urge its increase (1 Thess. 3:12; 4:9–10; 2 Thess. 1:3). We have also seen that each of the detailed instructional sections of the first letter concludes with the mandate for the congregation to take up the apostles' insights and to keep *encouraging* each other (1 Thess. 4:18; 5:11). The latter verse adds the notion of edifying or building up each other, famous from Paul's Corinthian injunctions (esp. 1 Cor. 14:1–5, 12, 26).

Whether or not the church is emulating the apostles' proclamation of the gospel message (1 Thess. 1:8), its members are replicating the apostles' fortification of congregations. The book of Acts focuses particularly on the unhindered spread of the word of the Lord, but it includes a surprising number of references to "strengthening" existing disciples and churches (e.g., Acts 14:22; 15:32, 41; 16:5; 18:23).[17] We find this same concern articulated in the Thessalonian letters: that the congregation be further "established" or "strengthened" in faithful and holy living (1 Thess. 3:2, 13; 2 Thess. 2:17; 3:3).

In short, the call to imitate the apostles' ongoing nurture of the Thessalonian church means that the Thessalonian sisters and brothers are to continue laboring hard at nurturing each other.

We have been rejoicing to find in Thessalonica a church progressing well. We have been delighting to read in the Thessalonian letters some positive praise and instruction. The apostles continue to work hard for them, albeit now at an unhappy distance. Especially with a congregation that is both young and progressing favorably, any forthright demands are juxtaposed with abundant encouragement and assurance. Congregations of a more recalcitrant kind may need stronger language

---

17  Alan J. Thompson, "Paul as Pastor in Acts: Modelling and Teaching Perseverance in the Faith," in *Paul as Pastor*, ed. Brian S. Rosner, Andrew S. Malone, and Trevor J. Burke (London: Bloomsbury T&T Clark, 2018), 17–30, esp. 18–22.

(Corinth and Galatia spring to mind), but God's diverse Scriptures model for us more than one mode of shepherding God's flocks.

Our final chapter turns to discerning what more we might learn about this triune God himself and how his chosen children and his appointed laborers can interact with him.

5

# The Living and True God

The Triune God Who Commences,
Continues, and Completes the Journey

PRIOR CHAPTERS HAVE ALREADY accentuated the role of the triune God in the Christian journey. God starts and sustains this journey, and he will bring it to a conclusion and proclaim judgment in favor of successful participants. My subtitle for this chapter attempts an alliterative summary of God's comprehensive oversight of every stage.

What do the Thessalonian letters contribute to our understanding of the identity and actions—traditionally the "person" and "work"—of this triune God? This final chapter considers how God is portrayed as the source of apostles' authority and believers' salvation. We also investigate what our letters teach us about praying to this triune God, which is a response to God and his work that these two letters clearly model and command.

## The Triune God

A simple search for mentions of Father, Son, and Spirit shows just how prominent they are in the Thessalonian letters. Names or titles or pronouns occur in roughly 58 percent of the letters' verses or 68 percent of their Greek sentences. This puts the letters among Paul's more God-saturated writings (see the excursus on the next page).

We consider here the persons of the Trinity in an order reversed from typical listings. I explain my logic as we progress.

**Excursus: Frequency of Trinitarian References**

Leon Morris notes how the Pauline letters refer to "God" more
than other parts of the New Testament—branding the apostle
"a God-intoxicated man."[a] A crude count of references to all
persons of the Trinity in Paul's letters, allowing for letter length,
suggests that their frequencies could be ranked as follows (the
letters fall into several clusters, presented here from the most
frequent mentions of "God" to the least):

Ephesians
Colossians, 2 Thessalonians
Romans, Philippians, 1 Thessalonians
2 Corinthians, Galatians, 2 Timothy, Titus
1 Corinthians, 1 Timothy
Philemon

The Thessalonian correspondence keeps heady company near
the top of the list. The two letters rank similarly if we narrow
our focus simply to God or to Jesus.

a    Leon Morris, *1 and 2 Thessalonians*, WBT (Dallas: Word, 1989), 11–12.

## The Holy Spirit

When it comes to the Holy Spirit in Paul's writings, the Thessalonian
letters fall below average. For denser teaching on the Spirit, we must
turn to Galatians, Ephesians, Romans, and 1 Corinthians (in that order).
The overt mentions in Thessalonians are so sparse that we can survey
them exhaustively. Each is theologically important.

The first two mentions correspond well with the popular perception
of the Spirit as facilitating conversion (1 Thess. 1:5–6). As we surveyed

in our opening chapter, our missionary authors happily recount how their gospel proclamation was not merely composed of human words but was accompanied by "power" effected by "the Holy Spirit" and by "full conviction." Confusion about whether the last term describes the preachers or their hearers arises because the celebration recalls the Thessalonians' resulting Spirit-induced joy. Those of us tempted to limit conversion to a cerebral assent of faith (e.g., Rom. 10:9) need helpful correction in noting how often joy and peace and more are linked with the Spirit (Acts 13:52; Rom. 14:17; 15:13; Gal. 5:22–23; cf. Col. 3:16).

In chapter 2 we explored the topic of holy living, concentrated especially in 1 Thessalonians 4:1–8. The topic sentence near the start of the passage concerns "the will of God, your sanctification [or holiness]" (4:3), and "holiness" remains the focus (4:4, 7). Unsurprisingly, the final warning in 4:8 draws attention to "God, who gives his *Holy* Spirit to you." Like the rest of the New Testament, the Thessalonian letters don't always include this adjective for God's Spirit; its inclusion here is telling. It's probably also a tacit reminder to these converts—who, like many contemporary Christians, have a Gentile heritage rather than biological Jewish ancestry—that they and we are inheritors of God's promises forecasting a new, holy, Spirit-fueled covenant people for his fame (esp. Ezek. 36:22–28 and surrounding verses).[1] The message of 1 Thessalonians 4:8 emphasizes Christian identity and behavior. Secondarily, the verse resonates with the widespread scriptural language of God's provision of the Spirit (e.g., Ex. 31:1–3; Num. 11:25; Isa. 44:3; Ezek. 36:27; 37:14; Joel 2:28–29; Luke 11:13; John 14:26; Acts 5:32; 15:8; Rom. 5:5; 2 Cor. 1:21–22; 5:5; Gal. 4:6; Titus 3:5–6; 1 John 3:24; 4:13).[2]

---

1   Gary S. Shogren, *1 & 2 Thessalonians*, ZECNT 13 (Grand Rapids, MI: Zondervan, 2012), 173–74; Jeffrey A. D. Weima, *1-2 Thessalonians*, BECNT 13 (Grand Rapids, MI: Baker Academic, 2014), 281–83.

2   Systematic theologians unpack the formalities of Trinitarian relations; see, e.g., Michael F. Bird, *Evangelical Theology: A Biblical and Systematic Introduction*, 2nd ed. (Grand Rapids, MI: Zondervan Academic, 2020), 682–86; John S. Feinberg, *No One Like Him: The Doctrine of God*, FET (Wheaton, IL: Crossway, 2001), 481–86.

"Do not quench the Spirit" is the usual translation of 1 Thessalonians 5:19. Perhaps to our surprise or disappointment, God's Spirit can be resisted and grieved (Isa. 63:10; Acts 7:51–53; Eph. 4:30). We need not guess at which elements of the Spirit's work are at risk of rejection in Thessalonica: the next verses and their instructions expand a concern not to despise prophecies but to test them. It is unclear whether the Thessalonians are too hesitant or too ready to trust such prophecies—compare the chaotic eagerness at nearby Corinth (1 Cor. 14:26–33). The remaining Thessalonian verses talk about testing "good" versus "evil," and the combined message of permitting prophecies and sifting the authentic from the inauthentic runs through the Bible (e.g., Deut. 13; 1 Kings 22:1–28; Jer. 23; 26–28; Matt. 7:15–23; 1 Cor. 12:10; 14:29; 1 John 4:1–3). The Thessalonians themselves will soon be spooked by false teaching, potentially via prophecy (2 Thess. 2:1–3).[3]

There is only a single overt mention of the Spirit in our second letter.[4] The apostles give thanks for God's work among the Thessalonian believers. It is worth reading the entire verse, which I space out for clarity:

> But we ought always to give thanks to God for you,
> brothers [and sisters] beloved by the Lord,
> because God chose you as the firstfruits to be saved,
> through sanctification by the Spirit and belief in the
>     truth. (2 Thess. 2:13)

There are three valuable observations to make. First, the Spirit's action in conversion mirrors what we have already noted and what we may well expect (cf. 1 Thess. 1:5). We have earlier observed how

---

3    On discerning the Spirit, see Graham A. Cole, *He Who Gives Life: The Doctrine of the Holy Spirit*, FET (Wheaton, IL: Crossway, 2007), 273–76 and the wider chapter. See also 246–47 on grieving the Spirit.

4    Gordon Fee's analysis also finds allusions to the Spirit in 2 Thess. 1:11 ("his power") and 2:2 ("a spiritual utterance," CSB mg.). *God's Empowering Presence: The Holy Spirit in the Letters of Paul* (Peabody, MA: Hendrickson, 1994), 67–79.

"being sanctified" can describe God's *initial* work in believers. Our verse here presents the Spirit's sanctifying work as a parallel description of God's choice in saving believers such as the Thessalonian Christians.

A second observation is unsurprising. As often in the New Testament, the Spirit's ministry is described in concert with others of the Trinity. All three are named here, as in the similar passage concerning salvation in 1 Thessalonians 1:4–6 and in the reasons given for holy living in 4:6–8.

Third, we once again see the close pairing of divine and human actions. The final phrase tells us that God's choice unto salvation is enacted through two means: through the Spirit's sanctifying work and through human belief in the truth. This does not require that the two means are equal or independent (see also 2 Thess. 1:11–12; 2:16–17; cf. Phil. 2:12–13). Yet both means are named, and translations capture this tension well whether they repeat the word "through" (CSB, NIV, NRSV) or emulate the Greek and express one "through" played out via both channels (ESV, NASB). The ensuing two verses continue this divine-human pairing. God called the Thessalonians through the "gospel" that the missionaries preached (2 Thess. 2:14). And the apostles' confidence in God's choice, calling, and faithfulness does not stop them from instructing human persistence (2:15).

We may be surprised at so few references to the Spirit, especially in letters emphasizing the start of the readers' faith journey. Scholars assure us that this is consistent with related writings; as Douglas Moo avers, "We look in vain for concentrated teaching in Paul about the Spirit."[5] As elsewhere in the New Testament, the Spirit operates more behind the scenes than in the limelight of center stage. Still, as Gordon Fee's celebrated study shows, even these few and fleeting mentions in Thessalonians "touch on most of the issues in Pauline pneumatology" and depict the Spirit shaping Christian life "from beginning to end."[6]

---

5    Douglas J. Moo, *A Theology of Paul and His Letters: The Gift of the New Realm in Christ*, BTNT (Grand Rapids, MI: Zondervan Academic, 2021), 610.

6    Fee, *God's Empowering Presence*, 40, 79–80.

*The Lord Jesus Christ*

If the Holy Spirit is barely mentioned, the second person of the Trinity is on high rotation. God the Son even marginally surpasses the many mentions of "God."

We might be surprised that only in the last two decades has detailed focus on the Christology of Paul's letters accelerated, but the results are now well assured. We are especially indebted to Fee's *Pauline Christology*.[7] As with Fee's book on Pauline pneumatology, this volume remains widely praised, and I eagerly draw on it. Fee focuses on who Jesus is, though we must extend his interest to observe also what Jesus has done. Another key reason for introducing Fee's works is his regular reminder that the two Thessalonian letters are among the first recorded words of the entire New Testament. He holds that Galatians was written later, and thus 1 Thessalonians—joined immediately by its stablemate—preserves the very first extant words about the Trinity! Fee is equally enthralled to notice how the letters' pneumatology and Christology are assumed without explanation or argument, suggesting that what we read here was well entrenched in the early church within two decades of Jesus's earthly ministry.[8]

Ben Witherington III notes that "Pauline christology has frequently been discussed under the headings of the prominent titles Paul employed—Christ, Lord, Son of God, Savior—and prominent analogies such as Adam and Wisdom."[9] Almost all of these are sparse indeed in our two letters. The label "Son" occurs only once, in 1 Thessalonians 1:10. That verse, and two occurrences in 4:14, give the only three stand-alone uses of "Jesus." Four times "Christ" appears on its own (1 Thess. 2:6; 3:2; 4:16; 2 Thess. 3:5), always to qualify some other concept (e.g., "gospel of Christ"); two further such qualifiers use the compound

---

7   Gordon D. Fee, *Pauline Christology: An Exegetical-Theological Study* (Peabody, MA: Hendrickson, 2007). His introductory chapter (esp. 10–15) outlines the history and paucity of research.

8   Fee, *Pauline Christology*, 31–33. He also proposes that the lack of detailed explanation concerning Jesus's identity is why these letters so rarely figure in Christological scholarship.

9   Ben Witherington III, "Christology," *DPL*[1] 100. Moo thoughtfully cautions that "title" is a potentially misleading descriptor. He favors the broader term "appellation." *Theology of Paul*, 362–63.

"Christ Jesus" (1 Thess. 2:14; 5:18). There is no overt labeling of Jesus as "Savior" (the closest language is in 5:9) and no obvious Adam or Wisdom Christologies.

The paucity of most key terms foregrounds the dominance of "Lord" and its forty-six appearances in eighty sentences. While sometimes clarified as "Lord Jesus" (10x) or "Lord Jesus Christ" (14x), the appellation occurs almost as often on its own (22x). Our two letters "punch above their weight." They constitute barely 7 percent of the words among the thirteen epistles associated with Paul, yet almost 20 percent of the occurrences of "Lord" applied to Jesus are found in these eight chapters. Whether we are interested in the theological development from the Old Testament's use of the term (especially the divine name, Yahweh, typically rendered "the LORD" in English Bibles) or in the complete submission owed to the triune God (following various "lordship" debates over salvation and discipleship), the Thessalonian letters provide disproportionate grist for our mill. Romans may highlight the importance of confessing that "Jesus is Lord" (Rom. 10:9), but at one-third its length, we see in Thessalonians the accolade "Lord" put into practice more often in total and nearly four times more frequently.

Many fine studies explore the significance that even here among the earliest New Testament writings—and without apology or explanation—Jesus of Nazareth is ascribed the titles, activities, and prerogatives of Israel's Deity. We see later in this chapter that, in tandem with God, divine grace and mercies are claimed from the Lord Jesus Christ, his authority is invoked, and prayers are offered to him. Such "early high Christology" sounds obvious to conservative Christians, and calling Jesus "Lord" is key evidence for prominent scholarly defenses of this crucial doctrine.[10]

Alongside passages where the Lord Jesus and God are invoked together in blessings and other prayers, it's equally powerful to note

---

10  Alongside Fee's *Pauline Christology*, recent staples include Larry W. Hurtado, *Lord Jesus Christ: Devotion to Jesus in Earliest Christianity* (Grand Rapids, MI: Eerdmans, 2003); Richard J. Bauckham, *Jesus and the God of Israel: "God Crucified" and Other Studies on the New Testament's Christology of Divine Identity* (Milton Keynes, UK: Paternoster, 2008).

matching descriptors ascribed to them independently. The first letter concludes with a prayer for the sanctifying work of "the *God* of peace," confident in his "faithful" sustaining of believers (1 Thess. 5:23–24). The second letter closes by beseeching peace from "the *Lord* of peace" (2 Thess. 3:16), having recently praised him as "faithful" in strengthening his people amid opposition (3:3). And while the earlier prayer of 1 Thessalonians 3:11–13 is addressed to both "our God and Father" and "our Lord Jesus," it's strictly the latter Lord who is asked to strengthen the Thessalonians' hearts in holiness, even though we have just seen later in that letter that the authors ask *God* for such sanctification. Similarly, the believers are sometimes called into God's glory (1 Thess. 2:12) and other times called toward Christ's glory (2 Thess. 2:14). The apostles comfortably apply the same vocabulary to either member of the Trinity. Many more examples of overlap can be demonstrated, shared within Thessalonians and shared between Thessalonians and the wider Pauline corpus.[11]

We have seen *that* the apostles focus heavily on lordship language for Jesus in these letters. It is good also to ask *why* they do so. Fee has already observed that the letters explain none of the Christological terms. Nor does the frequency here just reflect the normal frequency of "Lord." It's not that some church council is pending and here the authors pencil a précis of their doctrinal views. Nor dare we assume that Paul and his friends had an initial burst of enthusiasm or devotion for "Lord Jesus" in their early letters but then discovered focus groups responding better to different combinations and especially to "Christ" and "Christ Jesus" (even though the statistics could be read this way).[12]

11  Fee, *Pauline Christology*, 48–51, 69–73. Scholars rightly query whether "the Lord" throughout 2 Thess. 3 must refer to Jesus or might reference God. Virtually all accept Jesus: stridently, Gordon D. Fee, *The First and Second Letters to the Thessalonians*, NICNT (Grand Rapids, MI: Eerdmans, 2009), 313–14, 318–19; Weima, *1–2 Thessalonians*, 592. Dissent, favoring God as referent, is typified by Abraham J. Malherbe, *The Letters to the Thessalonians: A New Translation with Introduction and Commentary*, AB 32B (New York: Doubleday, 2000), e.g., 445.

12  Fee tabulates counts for all appellations (though there are minor errors in some summed totals). *Pauline Christology*, 26.

Rather, Fee helpfully reminds us of the city's background. After protracted conflict, Thessalonica currently enjoyed special treatment from the Roman Empire, and proclaiming the emperor as "Lord" preserved such perks.[13] It is precisely a charge of upsetting this balance that Acts records against the missionaries' visit to the city: disregarding Caesar's authority by "saying that there is *another* king, Jesus" (Acts 17:7).[14] The apostles are thus pastorally wise and encouraging when their follow-up letters heavily emphasize who is truly Lord of the universe. Modern populations continue to lurch between wildly varying perceptions of human authority and can benefit from the same lesson.

These early letters preserve for us other glimpses of Christological doctrines we might take for granted. Consider this declaration:

For since we believe that Jesus died and rose again, even so, through Jesus, God will bring with him those who have fallen asleep. (1 Thess. 4:14)

Along with 1:10, this is the only place where the name "Jesus" occurs without some other appellation. This may suggest that our authors are promoting an existing creedal statement or teaching. It affirms key stages in Jesus's interactions with humanity for salvation: his death, resurrection, and impending return. This verse occurs near the start of the primary teaching on Jesus's return (4:13–5:11), and that block concludes with a similar reminder of "salvation through our Lord Jesus Christ, who died for us" (5:9–10).

Of course, our short letters don't showcase every Christological detail. Yet we should include a few more that are relatively rare. Any neglect of Thessalonians might lead us to miss such insights.

13  Fee, *Pauline Christology*, 42; cf. 34, 56. Commentaries regularly introduce the city; most substantially, see Gene L. Green, *The Letters to the Thessalonians*, PNTC (Grand Rapids, MI: Eerdmans, 2002), 1–47; Weima, *1–2 Thessalonians*, 1–23.
14  Commentators helpfully show how the contents of the Thessalonian letters comport with this charge; see, e.g., Ben Witherington III, *The Acts of the Apostles: A Socio-Rhetorical Commentary* (Grand Rapids, MI: Eerdmans, 1998), 508; Craig S. Keener, *Acts: An Exegetical Commentary*, 4 vols. (Grand Rapids, MI: Baker Academic, 2012–2015), 3:2552–55.

John 3:16 has engraved on our memories that *God* loves his wayward world. Thessalonians names God's love for believers (1 Thess. 1:4;
2 Thess. 2:16; 3:5). We are familiar with *Jesus's* compassion on those
flocking to him during his earthly ministry. And John's Gospel speaks
of the incarnate Jesus loving his immediate disciples, Lazarus and his
sisters, and a special individual disciple. Yet I wonder if today we think
too little or too generically about Jesus's love for believers. There are
some proverbial mentions of "the love of Christ," but these don't overtly
specify whom he loves (Rom. 8:35; 2 Cor. 5:14; Eph. 3:19). It is hard to
find many clear statements that "Christ loved *us* and gave himself up
for us" (Eph. 5:2; cf. Rom. 8:37; Gal. 2:20; Eph. 5:25; Rev. 1:5). So even
though the language of 2 Thessalonians 2:13 sounds entirely obvious,
we ought not overlook its rare contribution in describing Christian
believers as "beloved *by the Lord [Jesus]*."[15]

Another all-too-obvious claim is that the Lord Jesus is the mecha-
nism by which God effects "salvation"—that foundational umbrella
term used by both lay believers and academic theologians (viz. sote-
riology). Romans 1:16 implies that it is the gospel message *concerning
Jesus* that is "the power of God for salvation." The most overt claims
are Hebrews 5:9, that the suffering-perfected Son "became the source
of eternal salvation," and 2 Timothy 2:10, extolling "the salvation that
is in Christ Jesus." So 1 Thessalonians 5:9 joins an elite epistolary short
list in confirming the way "to obtain salvation through our Lord Jesus
Christ."[16]

In chapter 2, we noted God's expectations of holiness. The Bible
regularly presents the pursuit of holiness as a human endeavor, with
God's holiness as our motivation and standard (esp. Lev. 11:44–45;
Heb. 12:14; 1 Pet. 1:15–16). This accords well with the "holy, holy, holy"
one enthroned in heaven (Ps. 22:3; Isa. 6:3; 43:14–15; Rev. 4:8; 6:10).

---

15  Commentators unpack why the phrase is valuable here; see, e.g., Weima, *1–2 Thessalonians*, 547–49.

16  Of course, there are occasional New Testament claims beyond the Letters, such as Matt.
1:21; Luke 19:10; John 3:17; Acts 4:12. The list lengthens when we include broader salvific
imagery (see the resources in chap. 1, 13n1); see, e.g., Mark 10:45; Acts 26:18; Rom.
3:24; Eph. 1:7; Titus 2:14; Rev. 5:9.

The triune God is also responsible for holiness, yet there are not many New Testament passages that transparently specify the divine agents of this sanctification. The Thessalonian letters join surprisingly short catalogues that identify each person of the Trinity at work: God the Father (1 Thess. 5:23 with Col. 1:22; Heb. 13:20–21), the Lord Jesus (1 Thess. 3:13 with Eph. 5:25–27; Heb. 2:11; 13:12), and the Spirit of holiness (2 Thess. 2:13 with Rom. 15:16; 1 Cor. 6:11; 1 Pet. 1:2). Many of these broader passages refer more to positional sanctification (traditional "justification") than progressive renewal (traditional "sanctification"). The Thessalonian verses affirm that Father and Son join the Spirit in contributing to progressive transformation as well as to initial conversion.

## God the Father

The issue of sanctification once again highlights how often the members of the Trinity work together. It can be difficult to spot their distinctive responsibilities—and sophisticated doctrines help us know how we should and shouldn't distinguish separate roles.

Similar complications arise when we see what terminology best applies to God the Father. We are right to worry about tying ourselves in knots trying to discern if "God" refers to one person of the Trinity or to all three. Fortunately, careful minds show that the term often does refer to God the Father, especially in the Thessalonian letters.[17] Seven times our authors clearly name "God the Father" (1 Thess. 1:1, 3; 3:11, 13; 2 Thess. 1:1, 2; 2:16), each time alongside, and thus distinguished from, "the Lord Jesus Christ." Most of the other mentions of "God" probably also single out the Father, although, frankly, it would hardly alter our understanding if these occasionally nominated the whole triune Deity.

It is perhaps this potential confusion or overlap in labels that sees parts of the evangelical church not giving due attention to God the Father. It is sometimes said that church traditions foreground a favorite person of the Trinity, accompanied by a runner-up. Often in reaction

17  Concerning Thessalonians, see Fee, *Pauline Christology*, 36–38; more generally, see Feinberg, *No One Like Him*, 456–58.

against underwhelming treatments of Jesus, evangelicals have pushed the Son to be front and center. Then, perhaps in an embarrassed rush to rectify neglect of the third person or because of unhappy or nebulous understandings of "God" (including notions of his wrath or mistreatment of his Son, some other objection, or simple uncertainty), the Spirit is promoted to second place. God the Father can lag behind at a distant or forgotten third.

I have approached this chapter in reverse Trinitarian order. I have saved discussion of the Father until last for several reasons. One is to ensure due attention, hoping to retain or restore appropriate reverence. Another is that much of what we can say about God the Father can be said only once we've understood God the Son; the Father is as much defined by the Son as the other way around.[18] Indeed, it is encouraging to see evangelical studies keeping an eye on *God* as the ultimate center of Pauline theology, of New Testament theology, and of biblical theology.[19]

Even if church language—including its musical language—sometimes errs more toward the Son or the Spirit, scholars reiterate the Father's centrality. This claim not only derives from Trinitarian theology but reflects the biblical terminology. Neil Richardson concludes for the Pauline writings that "throughout 'God' functions as origin, author, warrant and goal, 'Christ' as the agent or means."[20] Moo likewise corrects notions of Jesus acting autonomously, outlining "the way in which Paul describes what Jesus does—or, better, what God does in and through Jesus."[21]

---

18 Wesley Hill, *Paul and the Trinity: Persons, Relations, and the Pauline Letters* (Grand Rapids, MI: Eerdmans, 2015), 70–75; cf. Neil Richardson, *Paul's Language about God*, JSNTSup 99 (Sheffield: Sheffield Academic, 1994), e.g., 311–12. Like others, Hill insists on "a christological shape to God's character and actions [even] before the historically determinate Christ-event" (72).

19 Note the titles and subtitles (and contents), respectively, of Thomas R. Schreiner, *Paul, Apostle of God's Glory in Christ: A Pauline Theology*, 2nd ed. (Downers Grove, IL: IVP Academic, 2020); Schreiner, *New Testament Theology: Magnifying God in Christ* (Grand Rapids, MI: Baker Academic, 2008); James M. Hamilton Jr., *God's Glory in Salvation through Judgment: A Biblical Theology* (Wheaton, IL: Crossway, 2010).

20 Richardson, *Paul's Language about God*, 305; cf. 268. Richardson's analysis focuses on the seven uncontested letters.

21 Moo, *Theology of Paul*, 354.

So how are God the Father and his activity described in Thessalonians?

First, there are those many joint statements in which Father and Son act in concert. The two are together invoked in prayer. These prayers assume and confirm that both Father and Son are divine. (This isn't to deny divinity to the Spirit; these letters simply don't offer focused instruction on the third person of the Trinity.) Both Father and Son are a source of grace and peace (2 Thess. 1:2, 12). Both are asked to encourage and strengthen the believers to persevere in holy living (2:16–17 CSB, NIV). A similar sentiment appears in an earlier prayer, in which both Father and Son are also asked to facilitate the missionaries' return to their Thessalonian congregation (1 Thess. 3:11). Indeed, each letter opens with an affirmation that the teamwork of Father and Son together give description to the Thessalonians' church identity (1 Thess. 1:1; 2 Thess. 1:1). We have celebrated the "early high Christology" that such joint claims make for the Son. Neither should we overlook the Father's role in the formation of his church.

Second, our earlier investigations of conversion, holy living, and the denouement of current earthly existence (chaps. 1–3) each found God to be both the primary agent and primary beneficiary of such activities. And so we should praise God for his work in election and salvation, and we should persist toward his kingdom and glory.

We thus find that the Thessalonian letters reinforce much of our understanding of the Trinity. They especially foreground the prominence of God the Father and the lordship of Jesus the Son—important doctrines that would be less clearly attested without these epistles and that are further supported by a study of prayer.

## Praying to the Living and True God

Discussion of the Thessalonian letters' presentation of the triune God and his interactions with his world leads us naturally to consider how Christian believers interact with him. Letters to other churches occasionally disclose insights into what we might call public worship (e.g., 1 Cor. 11:17–34; 14; Col. 3:12–17). Thessalonians includes general comments about loving and encouraging one another (1 Thess. 4:10, 18; 5:11), about the place of prophecies (5:19–22), and about general conduct (5:12–15; cf. 2 Thess. 3:6–15). Alongside external behaviors, the most "religious" activity outlined in the Thessalonian letters concerns praying. The apostles emphasize praying through both direct instruction and indirect modeling.

It is hard to miss the prevalence of prayer in Thessalonians, regardless of the metric we apply.[22] Figure 3 offers a representation of passages relating to prayer. The apostles pray regularly for their flock. In turn, they instruct the Thessalonians likewise to be ceaseless in their prayers. These letters give particular insight into how we might pray for church members and for church leaders and missionaries. We also encounter extensive modeling for prayers of thankfulness, arguably more prominent here than in any other part of Scripture.

Figure 3   Passages concerning prayer in Thessalonians

### Praying to Jesus

Already we have been reminded that within the Pauline corpus, it is the prayers of Thessalonians that most prominently address not only God the Father but also the Lord Jesus Christ.

This claims more than just that Thessalonians helps to secure Jesus's divinity. It argues that these letters are "Exhibit A" for those who choose to pray and sing to Jesus. The letters are also a helpful challenge to

22 For example, Shogren conservatively identifies fifteen and thirteen verses of overt prayers, respectively, in the two letters—more than 20 percent. *1 & 2 Thessalonians*, 78n89. D. A. Carson's study of Pauline prayers offers eight chapters focused on specific texts. Three of these eight (chaps. 2, 3, 5) showcase the Thessalonian correspondence. Consequently, his Scripture index lists as many references for *each* of 1 Thessalonians and 2 Thessalonians as for Romans, and the two letters together earn more mentions than the two book chapters focused on Ephesians. *Praying with Paul: A Call to Spiritual Reformation*, 2nd ed. (Grand Rapids, MI: Baker Academic, 2014).

those of us who have imbibed too simplistically the notion that the *only* biblical way to pray is "to the Father, through the Son, by the Spirit."[23] This is not to engage the wider debate of Trinitarian praying but to demonstrate the relevance of Thessalonians for such discussions, which relevance is often overlooked.[24]

Richard Bauckham is correct that the number of biblical prayers to Jesus can be underestimated.[25] This sometimes stems from the narrow view that a prayer must be directly addressed *to* someone. Especially for those of us grammarians who look for occurrences of "Jesus" in the Greek vocative case, few present themselves (Acts 7:59–60; Rev. 22:20). But adding in third-person "prayer-wishes" and prayer reports and other variants greatly expands our list. Bauckham ends up with nearly a dozen primary examples and another dozen in secondary support. And the Thessalonian letters account for a full quarter of these!

These are all indirect in different ways. There are the minor blessings expressed in Jesus's name, especially at letter starts and ends (1 Thess. 5:28; 2 Thess. 1:2; 3:18). Then there are the three or four passages reflecting as many as seven stronger requests that the Lord Jesus would accomplish something (1 Thess. 3:11, 12–13; 2 Thess. 2:16–17; 3:5, 16 [2x]). Taken together, this evidence makes it very hard to deny that these "most likely reflect actual prayer practices."[26]

Two final comments: First, we have repeatedly noticed that the Lord Jesus is often invoked alongside God the Father. This says much about the letters' Christology. What more is added, then, when several of these prayers are addressed to the Lord Jesus *alone*? Second, if we have any sense that the Trinitarian persons carry any sort of ordering, we must

23 Such is the structure and teaching of Tim Chester, *The Message of Prayer: Approaching the Throne of Grace*, BST (Nottingham, UK: Inter-Varsity Press, 2003), e.g., 39, 64.

24 Sample discussions, concluding with somewhat different practical formulations, include Cole, *He Who Gives Life*, 84–87; Donald G. Bloesch, *God the Almighty: Power, Wisdom, Holiness, Love* (Downers Grove, IL: InterVarsity Press, 1995), 191–94. Both acknowledge prayers to Jesus, but they undercount them and make no mention of the dramatic Thessalonian examples. Nor have I found mention of the Thessalonian prayers to Jesus in recent systematic theologies.

25 Bauckham, *Jesus and the God of Israel*, 128–29.

26 Hurtado, *Lord Jesus Christ*, 139.

note how two closely related passages report their agents. There is little surprise about the ordering in a request made of "our God and Father himself, and our Lord Jesus" (1 Thess. 3:11). But our same apostles express a similar prayer to "our Lord Jesus Christ himself, and God our Father" (2 Thess. 2:16–17).[27]

## Praying Ceaselessly

There is no time of day and no time of life when praying is inappropriate. Christians recognize how obvious it is that we can (and should) pray at all times. Yet we might be struck by the way Thessalonians both *models* such a regular habit among the apostles and *instructs* it for believers.

Our eight chapters are full of the apostles' prayers for their flock. Even a brief list of the overt declarations of prayer helps to spotlight its prominence. The authors claim to pray regularly, and we see abundant evidence that they live out such claims:

We give thanks to God always for all of you, constantly mentioning you in our prayers. (1 Thess. 1:2)

And we also thank God constantly. (1 Thess. 2:13)

For what thanksgiving can we return to God for you? (1 Thess. 3:9)

We pray most earnestly night and day. (1 Thess. 3:10)

We ought always to give thanks to God for you, brothers [and sisters], as is right. (2 Thess. 1:3)

We always pray for you. (2 Thess. 1:11)

But we ought always to give thanks to God for you. (2 Thess. 2:13)

27  The similarities and differences are enthusiastically analyzed by Fee, *Pauline Christology*, 73–76 (largely repeated in Fee, *Thessalonians*, 306–8).

There are various other prayers, although these don't carry the overt qualifiers about being regular, habitual prayers. Such prayers and prayer-wishes are found in the traditional openings and closings of the letters and also at other major junctures (1 Thess. 1:1; 3:11–13; 5:23, 28; 2 Thess. 1:2; 2:16–17; 3:5, 16, 18; see fig. 3). Thus there is only a single chapter across the two letters bereft of obvious prayer, and prayer not only appears in the other seven chapters but thoroughly permeates them.

Just as the apostles expect the believers to imitate them in other elements of life and doctrine (see chap. 4), so too they expect believers to emulate their ceaseless praying. A famous string of short commands draws this to our attention:

> Rejoice always, pray without ceasing, give thanks in all circumstances. (1 Thess. 5:16–18)

The authors make additional injunctions to pray (1 Thess. 5:25; 2 Thess. 3:1–2), even if these don't attract the same "without ceasing" qualifiers.

These letters are soaked in the language and action and expectation of prayer. Throughout this book we have noticed how the Thessalonian letters keep an eye on every stage of the Christian walk. So it is no surprise that prayer becomes closely associated as a Christian characteristic. Nijay Gupta's commentary simply equates the new covenant community of Christian believers with "a people of prayer," which he elaborates this way:

> [Paul] is referring to a prayerful disposition where the believer always lives within the presence of God. . . . Paul tells the Thessalonians to be always-pray-ers so that they recognize the presence and goodness of God at all times and especially in difficult circumstances.[28]

As we consider some of these prayers in greater detail, we see even more starkly how pervasive they are and how they're pitched at every stage of a Christian's journey.

---

28  Nijay K. Gupta, *1–2 Thessalonians*, NCCS (Eugene, OR: Cascade, 2016), 118.

*Praying for Believers*

Students of Scripture can replicate lists of prayers through basic con-
cordance searching. What can be less apparent to casual readers is the
way these prayers substantially contribute to the underlying structure of
entire sections and chapters of the Thessalonian letters. Two examples
of structure suffice, one from each letter, before we turn to consider
briefly the content of the prayers.

The entire opening chapter of 1 Thessalonians is structured around the
apostles' thankfulness for their church. There is an initial report of gratitude (1:2–5 is a single sentence in Greek), followed by various further
grounds for thanksgiving (1:6–10).[29] The chapter thus revolves around
two primary statements that are causally linked: "We thank God always
concerning you" because "you became imitators of us and of the Lord"
(1:2, 6, my trans.). Whether or not the next prayer report is a continuation or resumption of the opening thanksgiving or a fresh outburst of
gratitude, 2:13–16 picks out precisely the same action and reason: "We
also thank God unceasingly . . . because you became imitators" of the
Judean churches (2:13–14, my trans.). The general tenor of thanksgiving
wraps up in final prayers (3:11–13) that just happen to raise the two main
matters addressed in the remaining chapters. Commentators regularly
identify this central prayer as a structurally significant transition.[30]

The second letter is structured nearly identically. It opens the same
way: "We ought to thank God always concerning you" (2 Thess. 1:3,
my trans.). Again, there follows a long list outlining the basis for this
gratefulness (1:3–10 is a single Greek sentence). As with the first letter,
thankfulness here is sparked by the Thessalonians' ongoing response
to God's work in them: for their increasing love, their perseverance,
and their ongoing faith despite opposition. (This persistent faithfulness
leads to further discussion of God's judgment at Jesus's return, which
we considered above in chap. 3.) Whereas the authors' thanksgivings
in 1 Thessalonians typically focus on the believers' imitation and pro-

29  Weima, *1–2 Thessalonians*, 79–80; cf. NET.
30  John C. Hurd, "1 Thessalonians 3:11–13: The Pivotal Importance of Prayer in the Structure
    of Paul's Letters," *Arc* 33 (2005): 257–80.

duce more praise, here in 2 Thessalonians the thanksgiving gives rise to additional prayer requests directed to God. The opening chapter concludes with a detailed report of such requests.

And where the thanksgiving and praise of 1 Thessalonians 1 is repeated soon after in 2:13–16, we find that the thanksgiving and prayer of 2 Thessalonians 1 is repeated soon after in 2:13–17. Again, "we ought to thank God always concerning you" (2:13, my trans.), and again, this leads to specific prayers that Jesus and God would encourage and strengthen the believers in the persistence they're called to. Again, these prayers summarize the opening concerns and then transition into the final chapter of the letter.

What can we learn about the *content* of praying for believers? The Thessalonians are praised for imitating the apostles, so we can be confident that the extended prayer reports are partly to provide additional teaching and modeling about what that first generation of believers might themselves pray for. No doubt contemporary Christians are also intended to learn from these first-century examples. Just as we have found the Thessalonian letters to address each stage of the Christian walk, we should be unsurprised that the Thessalonian prayers for believers likewise address each of these stages.

Certainly, the various thanksgivings are based on the Thessalonians' original response to God's election. We hear overtly of their election and the dramatic and powerful impact of the Spirit's work through the missionaries' preaching of the gospel message (1 Thess. 1:4–5; 2:13; 2 Thess. 2:13–14). That past impact continues to be reflected in the Thessalonians' present lifestyle as their faith, hope, and love continue to produce labors and perseverance (1 Thess. 1:3; 2 Thess. 1:3–4).

In turn, the specific prayerful petitions that the apostles continually offer to God for their congregation are concerned with the believers' persistence in this present lifestyle until the end of their current earthly journey. While not the sum total of the prayer, the opening line of the first petition in the second letter draws attention to this very issue of remaining worthy of God's election: "To this end we always pray for you, that our God may make you worthy of his calling" (2 Thess. 1:11).

Ensuing clauses beseech God to continue his work in the Thessalonians such that they might be glorified even as their lives bring glory to the name of the Lord Jesus (1:11–12).[31]

The parallel passage in the next chapter retreads the very same sequence (2:13–17). The missionaries repeatedly thank God for his effectual work in the past. They command the Thessalonians, "Stand firm and hold to the traditions that you were taught by us." And they ask that the Lord Jesus Christ and God the Father would encourage and strengthen the Thessalonians in every good work and word.

In addition to the passages we have already noted, 1 Thessalonians 3:9–13 also follows the same pairing: thankfulness for the past leads to prayers for the future (as well as ongoing ministry hopes for the present and near future).[32] Such a future orientation is captured neatly in the prayer that virtually concludes the first letter:

> Now may the God of peace himself sanctify you completely. And may your whole spirit, soul, and body be kept sound and blameless at the coming of our Lord Jesus Christ. (1 Thess. 5:23 CSB)

It is perhaps less often asked *why* letters like these include prayers. Are these not merely statements of fact that Paul and Silvanus and Timothy prayed for their churches? Of course these apostles prayed. We rely on first-person accounts like these, alongside third-person narratives like those in Acts, to confirm the fact of such praying and to furnish example content. But at least three further reasons can enhance our own praying.[33]

---

31  It is this combination of thanksgiving for the past and present and petitions for the future that likely explains why Carson devotes two chapters in *Praying with Paul* (21–44) to 2 Thess. 1 and even why he opens his study with such a focus.

32  Indeed, Carson's third study of prayers in Thessalonians focuses on this section (1 Thess. 3:9–13), and his presentation similarly emphasizes past, present, and future elements. *Praying with Paul*, 59–73.

33  Such reasons are occasionally surveyed in technical studies. Weima considers several purposes of thanksgiving reports. *1–2 Thessalonians*, 75–76. The following outline does not exhaust all possible reasons. For example, encouraging prayers serve also to reinforce friendship—a recognized epistolary genre whose traits pervade especially the first let-

First, knowing what others are praying can help us echo those prayers and join in thanks once they're answered. We start to detect God's hand at work through his servants' prayers, and thus we cannot presume merely on our own proficiency or fortune.[34]

Second, in keeping with so many emphases in these letters about imitation, the apostles continue to model for their congregation the kinds of prayers that the believers themselves can learn to pray. Do we consider that our own prayers might be exemplars that nurture other believers?

Third, there are further pastoral and rhetorical points at work. Reporting their prayers in general (in addition to recording some of their specific prayers) is one more way that the authors can demonstrate how much they love and care for their fledgling flock. It reinforces the kinds of values and behaviors that the apostles might elsewhere instruct. Indeed, it sets a challenge before the readers: to the extent that they are responsible for their upright conduct (alongside God's enabling), they are once again shown the kinds of godly outcomes their leaders promote. As Jeffrey Weima observes for the petitions in 2 Thessalonians 1:11–12, "There is nothing subtle or hidden about Paul's desires for the Thessalonian church."[35]

We can thus appreciate David Peterson's recognition that including these prayers and prayer reports in written letters not only serves some epistolary function but also contributes directly to the apostles' teaching and pastoral ministries.[36]

### Praying for Leaders

We are in more familiar territory when we look at prayer *requests*. The apostolic leaders twice give instructions that their congregation members should pray for them in their ongoing ministries. Of course,

---

ter; see David A. deSilva, *An Introduction to the New Testament: Contexts, Methods, and Ministry Formation*, 2nd ed. (Downers Grove, IL: IVP Academic, 2018), 467–68.

34 Carson outlines the profound merits of telling others what we pray for them, including thanksgiving. *Praying with Paul*, e.g., 66–68.

35 Weima, *1–2 Thessalonians*, 76.

36 David G. Peterson, "Prayer in Paul's Writings," in *Teach Us to Pray: Prayer in the Bible and the World*, ed. D. A. Carson (Exeter, UK: Paternoster, 1990), 87.

we must adapt these thoughtfully for contemporary use. The apostolic contributors are not local church leaders, who are identified only in passing (1 Thess. 5:12–13) with no specific prayer requests instructed for them. The apostles here serve a role similar to those who planted our churches or established our denominations. In at least a derivative way, they might give us insights into how to pray for modern missionaries—and the requests such missionaries might ask of supporters.

The clearest injunction comes toward the close of the second letter (2 Thess. 3:1–2). The church is to pray two things for the church-planting apostles: (1) that the word of the Lord would continue to work through their ministry, as it had among the Thessalonians, and (2) that they might be rescued from the "wicked and evil" (3:2). The tenor of apostolic ministry displayed in these letters gives us confidence that the latter prayer serves the former. These apostles seem to care little about physical effort and hardship; they care less for their own comfort than for the thwarting of any impediments to the gospel's spread. Our confidence is reinforced when we observe that the coming verses remind the Thessalonians and pray for them that they too would be guarded from the ploys of the evil one and would continue in love and perseverance (3:3–5).

There is another general injunction to "pray for us" (1 Thess. 5:25) that provides no further content. Perhaps the apostles seek for themselves the same godly persistence they have just called the Thessalonians to (5:12–22) or the godly outcome they have just prayed for the church (5:23–24) or both. This coincides tidily with the same emphases we've just seen when the authors do spell out the content of their request in the later letter.

The same emphases are also on display in the one line in which the apostles pray for themselves. In 1 Thessalonians 3:11, the apostles ask God and Jesus directly to facilitate their return to their Thessalonian friends. From elsewhere, especially the immediately preceding verses, we know that this concern to return is focused on the Thessalonians' spiritual growth and the roadblocks thrown up by Satan (2:17–3:10).

There's also the string of terse injunctions to pray: "Rejoice always, pray without ceasing, give thanks in all circumstances" (5:16–18). We must assume that "pray" extends to all the kinds of petitions surveyed above, both for leaders and for other believers. The calls to "rejoice" and "give thanks" bring us full circle to the matter of praying with thanksgiving.

*Praying with Thanksgiving*

The list above of overt "ceaseless" prayers consists of seven examples. Five of these are expressly focused on giving thanks to God. It is easy to concur with Witherington that "to judge from [1 Thessalonians] 3:9 and the thanksgiving sections in almost all Paul's letters, prayers of gratitude or thanks were a major part of his prayer."[37]

The abundant thanksgiving furnished in the Thessalonian letters is extremely valuable. Paul's wider letters *demand* that Christians should be swept up in gratitude. Prayers of thanks are typically commanded alongside other prayers, almost as some kind of corequisite (esp. Eph. 5:18–20; Phil. 4:4–7; Col. 3:15–17; 1 Thess. 5:16–18; 1 Tim. 2:1–2).[38] The Heidelberg Catechism likewise judges all prayer necessary "because it is the chief part of thankfulness which God requires of us."[39] There are many examples of Paul's own thankful prayers to explore, although these are habitually concentrated in the first paragraph or two of his letters. We have seen that the two Thessalonian missives match this practice, but their additional contribution is the sheer extent of these introductory thanksgivings and the ongoing recurrence of thanks later in the letters.

---

37  Ben Witherington III, *1 and 2 Thessalonians: A Socio-Rhetorical Commentary* (Grand Rapids, MI: Eerdmans, 2006), 154. So prominent is thanksgiving in the opening chapters of the first letter that scholars debate whether the opening thanksgiving formally extends throughout 1:2–3:13.

38  It is also significant that the vast majority of New Testament thankfulness language is concentrated in Paul's writings and that when it comes to actual commands, as David Pao confirms, "only in Paul does one find a call to be thankful" (though he also allows the possibility of Heb. 12:28). *Thanksgiving: An Investigation of a Pauline Theme*, NSBT 13 (Leicester, UK: Apollos, 2002), 15.

39  The Heidelberg Catechism, Q116, Christian Classics Ethereal Library, accessed November 2, 2023, https://www.ccel.org/.

We have variously noted that the apostles' thanks is grounded on God's work in choosing the Thessalonians and their subsequent favorable response. We have observed that such thanksgiving (1) identifies God as the source of gospel successes, (2) models the correct directing of gratitude, and (3) maintains the "bar" the apostles have set for the Thessalonians to meet.

## Praying with Confidence

When we stop to think or talk about prayer, we're confronted with the question whether human requests can ever hold sway over the divine God to whom they're offered. Even the briefest survey of Thessalonian prayers assures us that Christians are expected to pray and that God does promise to hear such human prayers.[40]

Thessalonians certainly combats any sentiment that prayer changes only the person praying. The prayers that start, pivot, and conclude each letter presuppose that the triune God is active among his believers. Our missionaries are foolish to request prayers if these don't contribute to God's mission (e.g., 2 Thess. 3:1–2). Whatever internal transformations may *also* shape people at prayer, Paul's team is confident to propose externally measurable outcomes (e.g., 1 Thess. 3:11; cf. 2 Cor. 1:10–11; Phil. 1:19; Philem. 22; Heb. 13:19). Witherington captures it this way:

> The numerous prayers in 1 and 2 Thessalonians reflect the deep and profound piety of the apostle to the Gentiles. They also reflect his belief that prayer changes things, or, better said, the God who has chosen to respond to and answer prayer changes things.[41]

Such confidence, from Paul's team and from us today, makes sense of the commands and examples of "ceaseless" praying that pervade both these letters.

---

40  Note the balance attempted by G. K. Beale, *1–2 Thessalonians*, IVPNTC 13 (Downers Grove, IL: InterVarsity Press, 2003), 242–43; Schreiner, *Paul*, 321–23.

41  Witherington, *1 and 2 Thessalonians*, 263.

As we summarize the letters' emphases on prayer, we might note the striking parallels with the prayer instructions and requests made in Ephesians 6:18–20. There, as throughout Thessalonians, we find calls to ceaseless intercession on behalf of God's holy people, including prayer for the bold proclamatory work of the apostles, especially when obstacles impede their gospel message. Further parallels with other Pauline prayers can be found and appreciated. Speaking with such breadth in view, it is significant that one summary from D. A. Carson touches precisely on the key points promoted by the concerns and the prayers of the two Thessalonian letters: many Pauline intercessions "are for the spiritual maturation of believers, for their growth in love and obedience to the gospel and [for] their perseverance to the end."[42]

---

42  D. A. Carson, "Paul's Mission and Prayer," in *The Gospel to the Nations: Perspectives on Paul's Mission*, ed. Peter Bolt and Mark Thompson (Leicester, UK: Apollos, 2000), 180.

Epilogue

# Excel Still More

A VOLUME SIMILAR TO THIS ONE captures well my own sense of the Thessalonian letters. Our authors remind the believers in Thessalonica "that God has chosen them and that as a result of that selection they must now live out the consequences of that choice and accept the privileges and responsibilities of the call into the kingdom of God."[1]

Our first three chapters in particular have highlighted the three tenses of salvation and how each tense is relevant to believers' immediate circumstances. God's past, present, and future works should color how the Thessalonians live today. These believers are already moving well in the right direction, which is celebrated and nurtured. There remains room to grow: they have not yet "arrived"—either at the peak of Christian maturity or at the end of the earthly journey. Both perspectives, and thus a large proportion of the Thessalonian letters, can be summarized under the title of this epilogue: "Excel still more" (1 Thess. 4:1 NASB 1995).

The modern church does well to seek insight from these past pilgrims. Some of the New Testament can be read as corrective, turning wayward congregations from wrong to right. Other parts are assumed to be models for contemporary believers, although without much overt warrant or homiletical control (e.g., Which behaviors of Jesus's disciples

---

1   Karl P. Donfried and I. Howard Marshall, *The Theology of the Shorter Pauline Letters*, NTTh (Cambridge: Cambridge University Press, 1993), 29. Donfried speaks here of the first letter, but much applies also to the second.

are prudent, and which are distasteful?). But the Thessalonian letters introduce us to a church already moving in the right direction, one that is openly praised as "an example" for other believers (1 Thess. 1:7). Of course, other churches also serve as positive exemplars, especially much of what we hear about Philippi and Ephesus. Yet the church at Thessalonica must certainly join them as prize exhibits, especially for churches composed of members who are younger in their faith and not far progressed in the journey. We might also add the apostles' own concern that all members of the church, stronger and weaker, have opportunity to hear their message (5:27).

And of course, we learn much more about the triune God, whose church this is. God is not a sporting coach who spots natural talent and then leaves athletes to compete without further training. Even less is God a sporting agent who's content that his client has qualified for the final, as if this is adequate achievement. Rather, God is keen to ensure that his followers endure in the long-distance event and that they continue to develop toward elite performances worthy of his reputation. Being selected to God's team is but the start of the journey, and participants need ongoing formation and encouragement.

The two Thessalonian letters contribute much of God's training for us participants. We have seen how the apostles used their first-century words to bolster the first-century church. And we have glimpsed how this first-century "training manual" remains relevant for God's contemporary participants. We gain confidence from positive comparisons and overlaps with other parts of the Bible, all producing a concordant voice. This in turn assures us of the veracity of the unique contributions the Thessalonian letters offer.

The Christian journey is obviously more arduous than a rosy epilogue might summarize. Many societies, including the Thessalonians' and ours, can be keen to take shortcuts and to minimize effort and commitment. (We commonly watch lazily from the sidelines and lionize those relatively few athletes, musicians, or vocational professionals who are *so* focused as to reach the heights of their fields and gain wider notoriety.) Our introduction included the call to consecration rather than complacency, and Karl Donfried's corresponding warning echoes well here:

> Then as now there are those who claim to be Christian but who assert that they are able to bypass, through a moment of instant "redemption," the long and tedious moral maturation required of the believer. Sanctification and hope are often excised as outdated and no longer relevant.[2]

We could well name also contemporary distaste for the perseverance related to these other virtues.

Leon Morris would add that in addition to disinterest in sanctification and holiness, many sectors of the church (and of society) have succumbed to a vacuous notion of "hope" with little substance or basis; "we have mostly reduced hope to mindless optimism."[3] The heavy emphasis in 1 and 2 Thessalonians on the guaranteed, victorious return of Jesus to bring judgment makes these letters a valuable antidote. A regular diet of prayer and thankfulness is much of what fuels endurance until that return, preparing us to be found ready for God's final verdict. Figure 4 combines prior images and shows something of the space our letters devote to these two topics: eschatology and prayer. Indeed, the passages without shading or texture in the visual representation are composed substantially of the apostles' concerns that their congregation be prepared for the parousia and their instructions on how to live while waiting for it. Christian behavior joins prayer and eschatology as key themes of these letters.

1 Thessalonians                              2 Thessalonians

| 1 | 2 | 3 | 4 | 5 |   | 1 | 2 | 3 |

Figure 4    Passages focused on eschatology (shaded sections) and on prayer (textured sections)

2   Donfried and Marshall, *Shorter Pauline Letters*, 110.
3   Leon Morris, *1 and 2 Thessalonians*, WBT (Dallas: Word, 1989), 97.

May our reading of the two letters to the Thessalonian believers and our grateful and faithful responses to God's past, present, and future works in us and in his world continue to enthuse and equip us to walk and to please God—and to excel still more—until the coming of the Lord.

# Recommended Resources

## Commentaries

Fee, Gordon D. *The First and Second Letters to the Thessalonians*. New International Commentary on the New Testament. Grand Rapids, MI: Eerdmans, 2009.

Green, Gene L. *The Letters to the Thessalonians*. Pillar New Testament Commentary. Grand Rapids, MI: Eerdmans, 2002.

Gupta, Nijay K. *1–2 Thessalonians*. New Covenant Commentary Series. Eugene, OR: Cascade, 2016.

Johnson, Andy. *1 and 2 Thessalonians*. Two Horizons New Testament Commentary. Grand Rapids, MI: Eerdmans, 2016.

Kim, Seyoon, and F. F. Bruce. *1 & 2 Thessalonians*. 2nd ed. Word Biblical Commentary 45. Grand Rapids, MI: Zondervan Academic, 2023.

Malherbe, Abraham J. *The Letters to the Thessalonians: A New Translation with Introduction and Commentary*. Anchor Bible 32B. New York: Doubleday, 2000.

Shogren, Gary S. *1 & 2 Thessalonians*. Zondervan Exegetical Commentary on the New Testament 13. Grand Rapids, MI: Zondervan, 2012.

Weima, Jeffrey A. D. *1–2 Thessalonians*. Baker Exegetical Commentary on the New Testament 13. Grand Rapids, MI: Baker Academic, 2014.

Witherington, Ben, III. *1 and 2 Thessalonians: A Socio-Rhetorical Commentary*. Grand Rapids, MI: Eerdmans, 2006.

## Theological Volumes

Fee, Gordon D. *Pauline Christology: An Exegetical-Theological Study.* Peabody, MA: Hendrickson, 2007.

Gupta, Nijay K. *1 & 2 Thessalonians.* Zondervan Critical Introductions to the New Testament 13. Grand Rapids, MI: Zondervan Academic, 2019.

Moo, Douglas J. *A Theology of Paul and His Letters: The Gift of the New Realm in Christ.* Biblical Theology of the New Testament. Grand Rapids, MI: Zondervan Academic, 2021.

Morris, Leon. *1 and 2 Thessalonians.* Word Biblical Themes. Dallas: Word, 1989.

Schreiner, Thomas R. *Paul, Apostle of God's Glory in Christ: A Pauline Theology.* 2nd ed. Downers Grove, IL: IVP Academic, 2020.

## Focused Studies

Carson, D. A. *Praying with Paul: A Call to Spiritual Reformation.* 2nd ed. Grand Rapids, MI: Baker Academic, 2014, esp. chaps. 2, 3, 5.

Kim, Seyoon. *Paul's Gospel for the Thessalonians and Others: Essays on 1 & 2 Thessalonians and Other Pauline Epistles.* Wissenschaftliche Untersuchungen zum Neuen Testament 481. Tübingen: Mohr Siebeck, 2022.

Marshall, I. Howard. "Election and Calling to Salvation in 1 and 2 Thessalonians." In *The Thessalonian Correspondence,* edited by Raymond F. Collins, 259–76. Bibliotheca Ephemeridum Theologicarum Lovaniensium 87. Leuven, Belgium: Leuven University Press, 1990.

Rainbow, Paul A. "Justification according to Paul's Thessalonian Correspondence." *Bulletin for Biblical Research* 19 (2009): 249–74.

Weima, Jeffrey A. D. "Infants, Nursing Mother, and Father: Paul's Portrayal of a Pastor." *Calvin Theological Journal* 37 (2002): 209–29.

# General Index

darkness, 13, 19, 37, 44, 66
David, 88
daylight, 19, 45
day of the Lord, 44, 45, 60, 62, 63, 71–72
death, 91
deSilva, David, 43
discipleship, 103
disorderliness, 42
dispensationalism, 71, 72
divine activity, 38, 84, 101
Donfried, Karl, 125
double predestination, 26
drunkenness, 45

edification, 48
*ekklēsia*, 51
elders, 94
election, 23–29, 115
Ellingworth, Paul, 1, 4
emotions, 90
encouragement, 29, 45, 46, 47, 82, 95
Erickson, Millard, 26
eschatology, 55, 56, 57, 63, 69, 125
evangelical church, 2, 7, 60, 92, 107–8
evangelism, 2, 77
every-member ministry, 93–96
evil, 27, 72–73, 100
expectation, 43–46, 95

faith, 17–18, 34–35, 61, 74, 99
family imagery, 79
fatherhood imagery, 79, 107–9
Fee, Gordon, 72, 100n4, 101, 102, 104–5
final judgment, 10, 29, 53, 71
Francis of Assisi, 92
friendship, 116n33
fruit, 34–35
funerals, 61
future tense, 30, 49, 56, 74, 116, 123, 126

generosity, 41, 51
Gentiles, 25, 85
glory, 104

God
  commission of, 83
  communicators of, 88–89
  displeasing of, 84
  as the Father, 107–10
  judgment of, 28, 56
  presence of, 20, 22
goodness, 35, 43, 100
gospel
  communication of, 15
  language of, 16
  message of, 84
  power of, 17
  preaching of, 115
grace, 24n19
gratitude, 35, 110, 114, 119–20
great tribulation, 70, 72
grief, 58, 61
groups, versus individuals, 25
growth, 21, 123
Gupta, Nijay, 35, 58n4, 75n23, 113

Heidelberg Catechism, 119
heresy, 2
Hill, Wesley, 108n18
holiness
  disinterest in, 125
  expectations of, 47, 82, 106–7
  as flourishing and visible, 33–37
  as habitual, 36–37, 99
  prayer for, 104
  value of, 20–23
holy kiss, 48–49
Holy Spirit
  conversion of, 98
  conviction of, 17
  power of, 99
  presence of, 22
  resisting and grieving of, 100
  sanctification of, 101
  as second place, 108
hope, 18, 34–35, 58, 61, 67, 74–75, 125
Horton, Michael S., 18n12, 23, 34
hospitality, 50–51
human authority, 105
humanism, 91

# Scripture Index

15:41 ..........95
16:5.............95
16:11–40......2
16:14 ..........24
17 ..............2
17:1–4.........25
17:1–9.........2
17:5.............25
17:7.............105
17:10–12......2
17:16–34......2
18:23 ..........95
20:28–29......88
20:28–31......88
20:31–35......93
20:32 ..........45
21:17–28:31..68n13
23:1.............84
24:16 ..........84
26:18 ..........106n16
28:15 ..........60

*Romans*
book of .......2, 5, 20, 25, 90n11, 98,
            103, 110n22
1:1–4 ..........16
1:9..............84
1:14–15 .......25n21
1:16............17, 106
1:18–32.......73
3:24............106n16
4:17............20
5:3–5 ..........68n13
5:5..............99
6:1–4 ..........20
6:15–23 .......20
6:16............90n11
8:4..............37
8:33............25
8:35............106
8:37............106
9................25
9:1..............84
9:11 ............25
9:14–29 .......28
9:22–23 .......26n24

10:9............99, 103
11:2............90n11
11:5............25
11:7............25
11:7–8.........28
11:28 .........25
12:1–2.........84
12:3–8.........94
12:13 ..........51
12:17–18......52, 84
12:18 ..........48
13:12–13......19
14:17 ..........99
15:1–7.........49
15:13 ..........99
15:16 ..........107
15:22–29......51
15:25–27......50
15:26 ..........51
16:1–2.........51
16:13 ..........25
16:16 ..........50

*1 Corinthians*
book of .......2, 3, 20, 39n8, 45, 90n11,
            95, 98
1:18............17
1:30............21
2:1–5 ..........90
3:16............90n11
4:4..............84
4:14–15 .......79
4:16............92
5:6..............90n11
6:2–3 ..........90n11
6:9..............90n11
6:11............21, 107
6:15–19 .......90n11
6:18............39
6:18–20.......39
9:13............90n11
9:16–17 .......25n21
9:19............80
9:19–23 .......52
9:24............90n11
10:14 ..........39n8

# New Testament Theology

Edited by Thomas R. Schreiner and Brian S. Rosner, this
series presents clear, scholarly overviews of the main
theological themes of each book of the New Testament,
examining what they reveal about God and his relation to
the world in the context of the overarching biblical narrative.

For more information, visit **crossway.org**.